The British
Oskar Schindler

By the same author
Active Goodness (2017)
Ian Fleming's Inspiration (2021)

The British Oskar Schindler

The Life and Work of Nicholas Winton

Edward Abel Smith

First published in Great Britain in 2023 by
Pen & Sword History
An imprint of Pen & Sword Books Limited
Yorkshire – Philadelphia

Copyright © Edward Abel Smith 2023

ISBN 978 1 39901 148 8

The right of Edward Abel Smith to be identified as
Author of this Work has been asserted by him in accordance
with the Copyright, Designs and Patents Act 1988.

A CIP catalogue record for this book is
available from the British Library.

All rights reserved. No part of this book may be reproduced or
transmitted in any form or by any means, electronic or mechanical
including photocopying, recording or by any information storage and
retrieval system, without permission from the Publisher in writing.

Typeset by Mac Style
Printed in the UK by CPI Group (UK) Ltd, Croydon, CR0 4YY.

Pen & Sword Books Limited incorporates the imprints of After
the Battle, Atlas, Archaeology, Aviation, Discovery, Family History,
Fiction, History, Maritime, Military, Military Classics, Politics,
Select, Transport, True Crime, Air World, Frontline Publishing, Leo
Cooper, Remember When, Seaforth Publishing, The Praetorian Press,
Wharncliffe Local History, Wharncliffe Transport, Wharncliffe True
Crime and White Owl.

For a complete list of Pen & Sword titles please contact:

PEN & SWORD BOOKS LIMITED
47 Church Street, Barnsley, South Yorkshire, S70 2AS, England
E-mail: enquiries@pen-and-sword.co.uk
Website: www.pen-and-sword.co.uk
or
PEN AND SWORD BOOKS
1950 Lawrence Rd, Havertown, PA 19083, USA
E-mail: Uspen-and-sword@casematepublishers.com
Website: www.penandswordbooks.com

For Georgina, from her grateful husband

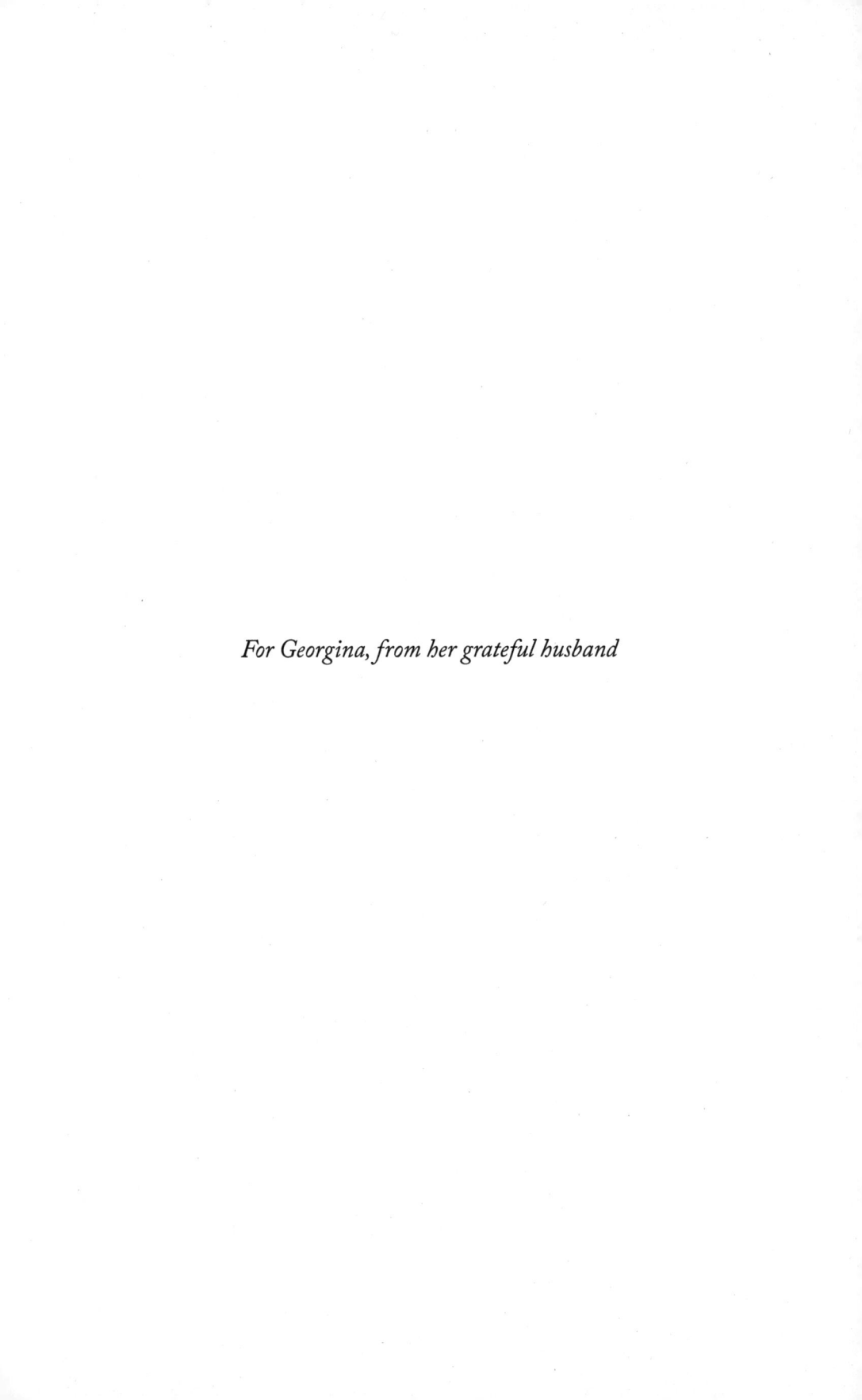

Contents

Acknowledgments		viii
Prologue		ix
Chapter 1	Introduction	1
Chapter 2	From Wertheim to Winton	6
Chapter 3	Rising from the Ashes	19
Chapter 4	A Different Winter Holiday	38
Chapter 5	Sightseeing	58
Chapter 6	Then There Were Three	66
Chapter 7	Occupation	84
Chapter 8	23:00 from Wilson Station	95
Chapter 9	The Duration	110
Chapter 10	Peacetime	122
Epilogue		135
Notes		139
List of Acronyms		148
Bibliography and Sources		149
Index		154

Acknowledgments

As a young(ish) author, it is always difficult to get work published, which is why I remain incredibly grateful to everyone at Pen & Sword for their continued support. Although it is a large team, I am particularly indebted to Jonathan Wright for taking me on in the first place.

There are many people who have generously given their time to me while researching this book, many of whom had to bravely recount unspeakable tragedy, and I am thankful to them all.

My father has painstakingly reviewed drafts of this book and provided me with much guidance throughout. I would like to thank him for all he has done for my books and for me.

My two daughters – one of whom was born in the middle of writing this book – continue to inspire me daily, while acting as a punctual alarm clock each morning. Finally, this book is dedicated to my wonderful wife, to whom I am forever thankful for marrying me.

Prologue

I had the pleasure of meeting Sir Nicholas Winton in 2009, briefly, as he opened a new building at my school. Having never before heard of Winton or his achievements, I was surprised to meet someone who was so unpretentious but dubbed by many as a 'hero' for saving hundreds of Jewish children from the Nazis at the start of the Second World War. Aged 99 at the time I met him, a matter of weeks away from his centennial birthday, the man's energy was incredible. He walked with a stick – although it seemed that this was something he carried as a prop rather than out of necessity. He appeared very steady on his feet, but insisted on linking arms with a rather attractive girl while she escorted him around the school.

After meeting Winton, I started to learn about his achievements. I had never stood face to face with someone who had saved someone else's life, and here was a man who had 669 to his name. What I later understood to be typical of his character, Winton was emphatic that his personal achievements had been exaggerated and there were many others who deserved the praise rather than him. The man whom everyone referred to as a hero was not only unpretentious, but also charmingly modest.

The more I learnt about Winton, the more there was to admire: his great sense of humour, his drive to help others, the fact that he had achieved so much after his rescue efforts during the war, and his near refusal to discuss this with anyone until the story became known.

It was hard to grasp the magnitude of his achievements and the impact that they have had on the lives of so many people. It is a remarkable fact that from the 669 children he saved in 1939, an estimated 10,000 descendants are alive today. Winton kept saying that he did not act alone, and in this Herculean effort, he had the assistance of many others. However, perhaps the real unsung heroes are the forgotten parents of the children who were saved. So desperate were they to protect their offspring that these brave men and women sent their beloved children to England in the knowledge that they would probably never see them again.

Hearing the children's recollections of leaving their families, the sheer courage of their parents hit home. It was only after having children of my own that I could truly appreciate the sacrifice these parents made. If, God forbid, I was ever in a similar situation, I fear that I would not be able to part with my daughters, no matter what the circumstances.

I have written this book to honour the amazing work of Sir Nicholas Winton and others around him who stepped up to save hundreds of children whose lives would have ended had they not acted. What became clear through my research is that Winton worked closely with several influential people to achieve his mission. Interwoven with this chronicle of his life, therefore, are the stories of some of those with whom he collaborated.

There are now several books available about Winton's life and accomplishments, and it is an honour to be able to add to this library of work in some small way.

Edward Abel Smith
2023

Chapter 1

Introduction

As the clock ticked past midnight on 1 July 1939, 10-year-old Vera Gissing was shaken awake as her train jerked violently over an awkward railway junction. Only one hour into her journey, for Vera this was a very strange time to be awake. The uncomfortable wooden benches in her carriage were crowded with children between the ages of 3 and 15, although it was hard to tell where the others were sitting in the pitch dark.

Vera was excited for her adventure, but she found it strange that her parents were not with her, and in her compartment, there were no adults. As the black countryside raced by, the children could only just make out the shapes of trees as the train screeched its way out of their home country, Czechoslovakia.

Although inevitable feelings of loneliness engulfed Vera and her companions as they travelled without their families – other than a few lucky ones who had brothers, sisters or cousins with them – the children were not alone. They were on one of eight such trains, hurtling from Prague, through Germany to the Hook of Holland, and then over the North Sea by boat to Harwich before boarding another train for London's Liverpool Street station. Vera was one of the group of 669 children making this journey over the space of four months in 1939.

All these children came from different backgrounds; few of them knew each other and they had little in common, but what they did share was not being aware of exactly where they were going, and more importantly, why they were making the journey. They certainly had little idea that they would most likely never see their parents again. Nor would they ever see any of the 15,000 other children from their country who were not chosen to be on one of these trains. The reason – over the next six years, 15,000 children and 144,000 adults were brutally murdered for having one thing in common: being Jewish.

Sixty-three years later, on 27 January 2001, now aged 73, Vera addressed a large audience in Central Hall Westminster, London. The international day of commemoration known as the Holocaust Memorial Day takes place on this date every year. During her speech, Vera recalled the first meeting with her new foster mother when she stepped off the train at Liverpool Street station in 1939: 'Her first words [to me] were, "You shall be loved." And those are the most important words any refugee child needs to hear,' she told the audience.[1]

Vera was on stage to introduce a man called Nicholas Winton as the special guest for the event. Unbeknown for many years to her and the other children, he was the man who had helped organise for her to be on that train. 'As one of the child refugees from Prague,' she said, 'I owe my life to Nicholas, but he could not have succeeded without the help of others.'[2]

Much has been reported and written about Winton. The common myth that he worked alone to organise the escape of Vera and her companions from occupied Czechoslovakia, dodging Nazi persecution, is so far from the truth that Winton himself spent much of his later life trying to rectify this misconception. In many of his speeches, he made it clear that recognition should also go to other people, commenting, 'In a way, I shouldn't have lived so long to give everyone the opportunity to exaggerate in the way they are doing today.'[3]

Like Winton, all of these 'other' people were just as modest, but probably the reason they escaped the attention of those writing the history books is that the vast majority died long before the story of their immense work become public knowledge. It was not until 1988, forty-nine years after the rescue took place, that their story was really told. Winton's wife, Grete, was carrying out the unenviable task of clearing out their attic when she found an extraordinary scrapbook, in which was recorded the details of Vera and her parents, and the names of all the other children that her husband had helped to rescue.

Not sure what to do with such a remarkable piece of history, Winton and Grete offered the book to Elizabeth Maxwell, the wife of controversial media giant Robert Maxwell. Elizabeth was one of the leading Holocaust researchers in the world, and Winton felt that his scrapbook could perhaps help with her work in tracing families torn apart by the terrible events orchestrated by the Nazis.

The scrapbook made its way around several prominent media and research individuals before landing on the desk of the producers of the BBC television show *That's Life!* Winton was invited to sit as part of the studio audience for the recording of one episode of the programme during which the elegantly professional presenter Esther Rantzen was going to reveal the story that was held within the scrapbook.

'These children would have been killed by the Nazis,' Rantzen announced to the camera as she flicked through the book, 'but in fact they were saved by an English stockbroker called Nicholas Winton.' As the camera panned across the audience, it rested on an elderly lady, who was visibly emotional.[4]

Reading from the autocue, telling the audience that this lady was Vera Gissing, Rantzen explained that only when the television show had contacted her the week before, had Vera learned some of the details about her escape. 'I had tried really hard to find out who had rescued us,' a different presenter read out on behalf of Gissing. 'I had even tried the Archbishop of Canterbury to see if he knew, but I drew a blank. I would very much like to meet Nicholas Winton to thank him for saving my life.'[5]

When Rantzen revealed that the man sitting to her right was in fact Nicholas Winton, the person who had arranged her rescue, Gissing seized his hand before reaching over to embrace him warmly. While the other audience members gasped and then applauded, Winton and Gissing exchanged short pleasantries, as they both wiped tears from their eyes. After introducing two more of Winton 'children' who were sitting around him, the television show came to a close.

However, this was not where Winton's time on *That's Life!* ended, as an appeal went out for as many as possible of Winton's rescued children – now middle-aged adults – to come forward to identify themselves. Invited to a later recording of the show, as Winton and his wife were sitting in the audience, it was now that one of the most amazing events of British television took place.

'Can I ask, is there anyone in our audience tonight who owes their life to Nicholas Winton,' Rantzen enquired, 'and if so, would you like to stand up, please?'[6]

All around Winton, nearly thirty men and women stood up and started applauding as their rescuer also stood up and looked behind him at all of their faces. Wiping away tears from his eyes once again, Winton sat down as the enthusiastic applause continued.

From that day onwards, Winton's life would never be the same again. What followed was a queue of dignitaries desperate to show recognition to this remarkable man, not least, because it had taken almost fifty years for his story to become publicly known. Presented with the highest Czech award, the Order of Tomáš Garrigue Masaryk, in 1998, a knighthood followed in 2003. That same year, he walked the red carpet with the likes of presenting duo Ant and Dec and British boy band Blue, to receive an ITV Pride of Britain Award.

As the tsunami of praise poured down on Winton, the story of his work in 1938 and 1939 became more and more exaggerated. Despite his attempts to put the record straight, the tale took on a new direction altogether. Newspapers endorsed inflated accounts of

Winton's part in the rescue. Headlines such as 'Sir Nicholas Winton single-handedly saved 669 Jewish children from the Holocaust' from *The Independent* still appear in newspapers today.[7]

However, the reality of this rescue story is rather different. Arguably even more remarkable, it is a story of the coming together of amazing people – all from different sectors of society – with one single goal in common: saving the lives of innocent children. Those involved included a teacher, a diplomat, a travel agent, a spy, a British Cabinet minister, the son of a vicar, a man on the run and a PhD lecturer. Each of these individuals deserves equal recognition and praise for their bravery and dedication, and the sacrifices they made to save Vera and so many other children.

The intention of this book is not to dilute the notable achievements of Nicholas Winton, who fully deserved all the awards and accolades he was rightly given. To have saved one child's life should warrant this level of recognition, let alone saving the lives of nearly 700. However, it is important to relate these events accurately, not only to show the accomplishments of others, but also to correctly praise Winton for his role in this story.

The book follows Winton's life, with a particular focus on the events of 1938 and 1939, but it also highlights several other key characters whose actions were integral to this operation.

Chapter 2

From Wertheim to Winton

Being of German heritage within Britain in the early twentieth century was an uncomfortable position to be in, to say the very least. Even the Saxe-Coburg and Gotha family – more commonly known as the Royal Family – changed their name to the House of Windsor, with the *Manchester Guardian* reporting that the Royals were 'Relinquishing the Use of All German Titles and Dignities', which included all 'Degrees, Styles, Dignities, Titles and Honours of Dukes and Duchesses of Saxony and Princes and Princesses of Saxe-Coburg and Gotha, and all other German Degrees, Styles, Dignities, Titles, Honours and Appellations'.[1]

Outside of royalty, with the mounting tension in Europe, culminating in the beginning of the Great War in 1914, Rudolf and Babette Wertheim, of German descent and living in Britain, were being ostracised from society. When their second child, Nicholas (Nicky) George Wertheim, was born on 19 May 1909, tensions were only starting to boil over. Nicky and his sister Charlotte, born in 1908 and known as Lottie, were well sheltered from the societal frictions by their parents. However, by the time their younger brother, Robert, known to all as Bobby, was born six years after Nicky in 1915, war with Germany was rife and things were tough for the Wertheim family. Their mother recalled that many of their local friends in Hampstead refused to speak to them until the Armistice in 1918. Such was the anti-German feeling that Rudolf followed the example set by the Royals, and swapped the family name from Wertheim to Winton.

Rudolf's parents, Nicholaus and Charlotte Wertheim, were German-Jewish immigrants who had moved to Britain in the 1850s from a town near Nürnberg (Nuremberg), 170 kilometres north of Munich. A successful businessman working in the bustling British capital, Nicholaus had become a British citizen in 1868. After having initially settled in Manchester, the couple travelled south to London and purchased a house in Hampstead in the 1870s.

In 1877, eleven years after their marriage, Nicholaus and Charlotte welcomed their first child, Bruno. He was followed by Sasha, born in 1879, Rudolf – Nicky's father – in 1881, and finally, Hannah (although her birth date is not known).

Despite living a comfortable life, tragedy struck the family in 1905, when both parents died within a few months of each other. Along with his siblings, the 24-year-old Rudolf struggled to come to terms with the loss of both parents within such a short space of time. The family home in Hampstead, with all its parental memories, became too much for Rudolf to face, so he travelled to Germany two years later, in 1907, where he lived for a few months.

It was in Germany that he met Babette, known to all as Babi and later, Barbara, who was a few years younger than he was and, in his eyes, a real beauty. The two fell instantly in love in a whirlwind romance and were married the same year. Babi came from a well-respected family in Nürnberg, where Rudolf's family had also dwelt for many generations. The medieval city was the site where Jews had first settled in Europe in the twelfth century, although – like so many times to follow – they were ostracised and only tolerated if they kept to themselves, while of course paying extremely high taxes. Although they were of Jewish origin, there is little evidence that the Wertheim family actively practised the religion. Their granddaughter, Barbara Winton, commented in 2014 that, as a family, 'they did not attend synagogue or use any obvious Jewish religious rituals at home'.[2] In fact, all three of Rudolf and Babi's children were baptised into the

Church of England in 1916, although this may well have been for the sake of fitting into British society.

Moving back to Britain later in 1907, Rudolf and Babi lived in their late parent's house, which had been bequeathed to Rudolf, despite him not being the eldest sibling, which would have been more customary.

Winton recollected in an interview in August 1990: 'We had an enormous house in Hampstead, which previously belonged to my father's parents. It was a twenty-roomed house, with a full-size billiard table.'[3]

The relative luxury of a large house – which today has been converted into nine flats, housing over twenty people – came with four members of staff: a cook, two maids and a nanny. Armed with her notebook, each morning the cook would meet with Babi to discuss the day's menu. For Winton's mother, this was the closest she would ever get to actually preparing or cooking food. With the nanny responsible for helping to raise the three children, the two maids ensured the house remained pristine. Despite the opulence, Winton believed, 'We weren't, by any means, rich … our class was, I suppose, moderately middle class.'[4] It is likely that what he really meant was that although they lived a financially secure life, the family did not mingle in the upper-class circles of British society.

Winton was 5 years old when, on 28 June 1914, Gavrilo Princip fired two shots from his .380 calibre pistol, fatally wounding Sophie, Duchess of Hohenberg, and her husband, Archduke Franz Ferdinand of Austria. This sparked the start of the First World War, at the end of which the Russian, Ottoman, German and Austro-Hungarian empires collapsed. Many countries formerly under their control became independent, including Czechoslovakia and Poland.

For Winton and his sister (their younger brother was not yet born), this was a time of great excitement, many times being woken in the middle of the night by their parents, when they would play a game of who could get to the cellar the quickest. Although bombs were falling all around their house from the deadly German Zeppelins – horrifying rigid airships used to drop explosives over Britain – Rudolf and Babi were able to shelter their children both physically and mentally from the destruction around them. During this period, Babi received the great news that she was expecting her third child (Bobby), who completed the family.

Although happy with his family, this was a dark period for Rudolf. Desperate to serve his adopted country, he volunteered to join the army, but was rejected. His German background was given as the reason, and with that, the opportunity to fight was gone. Ablebodied men such as Rudolf who did not serve in the military after the outbreak of war were instantly classed as cowards or, even worse, traitors. Women would walk up to such men, clearly distinguishable in their civilian clothes, and thrust a white feather into their hand. Such embarrassment for Rudolf was too much, especially as he was already considered an outcast because of his heritage, and despite no real change to his physical life, his health began to deteriorate. Compromise was eventually possible when he was allowed to join the Pioneer Corps, a light engineering unit that would later merge into the Royal Logistics Corps. While they had been responsible for the digging of the infamous Western Front trench network, Rudolf was classed among men 'not healthy enough to serve on the front line'. The sad irony was that by the end of the war, Rudolf's health had deteriorated so rapidly that had he been eligible to join up to serve abroad, he would not have been accepted.

In 1916, as the strain of conflict engulfed the nation, as an innocent 7-year-old, Winton started his schooling, attending the local University College School (UCS) in Frognal, Hampstead, housed in an imposing redbrick four-storey mansion. Founded in 1830 by philosopher and utilitarian Jeremy Bentham, the school was a place that encouraged its pupils to grow and develop at their own pace rather than having a rigid learning structure imposed upon them. Even the school's motto, *Paulatim sed firmiter*, Latin for 'Slowly but surely', epitomised this.

Though his new school was a mere three-minute walk from home, Winton was immediately unhappy, being treated as somewhat of an outsider. Given his German heritage, his friendship group was limited to those who were in a similar situation to himself, a perceived foreigner. Despite feeling like an outcast, Winton made friends with a pupil called Stanley Murdoch, who happened to live opposite him and became his closest friend. He would spend many happy hours at Stanley's family home, playing endless hands of cards. Stanley's mother was kind and welcoming to her son's new friend and would often join in with the games. For Winton, Stanley was everything a friend should be: funny, loud and always smiling. Their friendship only grew closer as the boys got older, to the point where they were almost inseparable.

What could have been a disaster for the friends turned into a great opportunity when Stanley announced that he was moving out of London. He had heard of a new school opening in Buckinghamshire, 80 miles north of London. Stowe School, an all boys' establishment, would have the pupils living in the magnificent Grade I listed country house, the former home of the Temple-Grenville family. The family had been forced to sell the estate in 1921 due to financial difficulties, including the 400-acre sprawling landscape garden designed by Capability Brown.

Murdoch was desperate to go to Stowe School to escape the monotony of Hampstead, but he wanted his best friend to go with him. Money was not an issue for the Wintons, so when their son broached the subject of changing school, his parents were happy to oblige. They contacted the headmaster, J.F. Roxburgh, a 35-year-old Scottish classics scholar. Known to all as simply J.F., he was a man who would be hugely influential to all the pupils he taught. Brought up in Edinburgh, J.F. had spent his younger years heading south, from Scotland to Liverpool, then down to Cambridge before settling in Surrey, and moving on to Stowe School.

The Wintons took to J.F. from the minute they met him. Like Rudolf, he had not only been turned down for military service in the Great War but had also been in the same regiment, serving on the front line in 1918, where his bravery was recognised when he was mentioned in dispatches. Many of J.F.'s pupils went on to have notable careers and some became famous, including the revered author Evelyn Waugh and actor David Niven (the latter attended Stowe School with Winton).

When asked by Rudolf and Babi what he expected of his pupils, J.F. replied that a good student would leave Stowe School being 'acceptable at a dance and invaluable in a shipwreck'.[5] Winton was to join Grenville House, managed by the charming housemaster Mr Clarke, who would also be a massive inspiration for Winton.

Consequently, after having spent seven years at University College School and his whole life in London, Winton moved to Stowe School in 1923. Today, the school's website, under 'notable alumni', describes Winton as having been 'one of the school's very first pupils when it opened in 1923 with under one hundred boys in total'.[6] It required a lot of adaptability for Winton to move from a well-run, established school such as UCS to one that was just opening and somewhat making up rules as they went along. Being neither good at sports nor academic, it would be understandable if Winton's time at Stowe School were less than remarkable. In fact, he kept himself busy with a whole host of unusual activities, the likes of which J.F. would only encourage.

Possibly his most bizarre passion was pigeon fancying – the art of collecting and breeding pigeons. Erecting his own pigeon lofts within the school grounds, Winton had an assemblage of sporting and flying birds of which he was immensely proud. While out running or walking with friends, he would take some of his stock and release them to find their way back to their cages. Naturally, he grew very close to his unusual pets and was devastated if any of them should die. He wrote to his parents in June 1925 that 'one of my pigeons is dead and I am very sad about it', before commenting a few days later, 'I had more bad luck. Another of my birds is dead.'[7] When he was not enjoying the company of his feathered friends, Winton would often be seen horse riding on the estate, or fencing. While he would dip his toe into some more conventional public school activities such as playing rugby – where he captained his side and was an integral try-scorer – and watching cricket, Winton invested his true passion in less mainstream hobbies. He had mixed experiences with horse riding, and after an accident involving a galloping horse and a low-hanging branch, he would understandably only rarely don his riding boots again.

Despite his limited success in the fields of equestrianism and ornithology, Winton became particularly competent in fencing. In an interview in 1990, he recalled: 'I was told that if I didn't play cricket, I'd have to fence, which was one of the only good things that happened to me in my early life, because I became a very good fencer.'[8] He was not exaggerating in the slightest and as an indispensable member of the eleven-man Stowe School fencing team, he helped log a record unbeaten season in 1926, when the team won all five of their matches against Oxford University, University College London, and Eton, Harrow and Westminster schools. If the Second World War had not interfered with the plans for the 1940 Olympic Games, Winton would most likely have made it into the British fencing team, having spent many years actively training for the event. He proudly commented while being interviewed by film director Matej Mináč that, with his brother, 'We founded the Winton Cup – an annual competition, which is now the largest fencing event in Great Britain!'[9] At the time of writing, the Winton Cup, divided into three categories – cadet, senior and veteran – is still a hotly contested annual competition.

As is custom in British boarding schools, a talent for sport – no matter how exclusive it might be – gave pupils a certain kudos over others, meaning Winton was never an unpopular boy, despite his off-the-beaten-path activities.

Academically, Winton's records were far less impressive in most of his subjects and his results were often below par, except for maths, at which he was rather good. However, he was a determined young man and made conscientious efforts to improve in the classroom. This was enough to satisfy his teachers – most importantly, J.F. Winton thought it crucial that he was not bottom of his class and when one teacher, Mr Heckie, commented that he felt he was more obsessed with his marks than actually learning, Winton commented in his diary, 'I will make a great effort so he never has need to say this again!'[10]

Winton was generally content with life at Stowe School but he remembered the time as an unhappy one, not least because he often thought of the school holidays as the highlights of his year. He always pined to be back at home with his parents and two siblings. Part of his enthusiasm for fencing was the fact that it allowed his parents to come to watch him in matches. His homesickness meant that he was reluctant to make new friends, and could count on one hand those that he truly valued, so he mostly spent his time alone or with Stanley Murdoch. So although it had been Winton's choice to move to Stowe School, being away from home did not suit him in the slightest.

Relief from Stowe School came in 1926, when, aged 17, he finished school for good. He had joined as a boy and was leaving as a man. Outside of self-taught knowledge of birds and his ability to defend his honour with a fencing sabre, he had gained a strong set of ethical beliefs. He also endorsed his religious faith by being confirmed as a Christian at the age of 16. To mark the occasion, J.F. gave Winton a copy of *The Book of Common Prayer*, which he kept his whole life.

* * *

Winton left with his School Certificate, having passed English, Maths and Physics, but with unimpressive grades in all his other subjects. Keen to attend university, he looked into taking evening classes to top up his marks and believed this was a viable option for him. However, his father was eager for his eldest son to start working immediately. Rudolf had decided after the Great War not to re-enter the banking fraternity but instead chose to go into the glass business, importing goods from Czechoslovakia, a country where his son would later rightly become known as a national treasure. Unfortunately, the glass business was not a successful commercial venture, and the family soon found themselves in a tight financial position.

Because of this, Rudolf was very persuasive in that Winton should start earning a salary as soon as possible, especially because of the value of the price tag attached to his public school fees. When Winton told his father that he planned to take up further education in order to qualify as a solicitor, Rudolf simply replied, 'You have to be very clever to be a solicitor.'[11] That was the last Winton thought of a career in law and instead he focused on financial services, his father's industry of choice for him, knowing that an occupation in banking could make good money. 'Father was very keen that I should become a banker,' Winton recalled somewhat resentfully.[12] Although he made a career for himself as a young man, the industry was never something he was truly passionate about and this would manifest as he grew older.

With the help of family connections, Winton secured a clerk training programme with a bank called Japhet in early 1927. For two years, he enjoyed a routine of working eight hours a day in the bank, meeting his father for lunch and socialising with his mostly male friendship group in the evening. While working, Winton was able to continue fencing at Salle Bertrand in London, where he competed successfully against other members, most notably Oswald Mosley, who had been the youngest sitting Member of Parliament before going on to be head of the British Union of Fascists. To hear the views of someone with such opposing ideologies to himself was a novel and unsettling experience for Winton.

Despite working in the lucrative financial sector, pay was not enough to sustain Winton in London alone, so he very happily moved back into his parents' house. He remembered the time incredibly fondly, not least because, when aged 19, he began his first relationship, with Elizabeth O'Malley, who was two years his junior and a girl of natural beauty. Elizabeth had been orphaned as a toddler and was now living in the care of one Mr Sala, who lived on the same street as the Wintons. Having spent his teenage years at an all boys' school, like many of his peers, Winton was somewhat awkward around members of the opposite sex. However, he summed up the courage to ask Elizabeth out, and he courted her for a straight six weeks.

The relationship came to an abrupt end when Winton was sent to Germany as part of his training contract. Although he had only spent a short amount of time with Elizabeth – enjoying dinners together, trips to the cinema and even a visit to his old haunting ground of Stowe School – as his posting abroad could last up to three years, he decided he would try to remain in a long-distance relationship with her. 'I shall be sorry to leave Elizabeth,' he wrote in his diary. 'We have got very friendly in a very short time.'[13]

Winton left for Germany on 20 May 1929, travelling to Berlin with his mother and sister by ferry and train. His Aunt Ida and her son greeted them at the station in the German capital. What followed for Winton was a blissful two weeks with his family, exploring the city, enjoying the local cuisine and attending the opera. His father joined them a few days after their arrival, to help settle his eldest son into his new life and new job. When his parents and sister left to return to London, Winton found the parting particularly difficult, and missed his family enormously.

Winton's posting was in the banking division of L. Behrens und Söhne, a Hamburg private trading company, run by the descendant of one of the firm's founders, a Jew named George Eduard Behrens. In 1938, Behrens left his post and fled the country, and was replaced by a Nazi-approved Aryan manager.

Working under Dr Eberstadt, Winton toiled long days from 9 am to 7 pm, with a two-hour lunch break to interrupt the monotonous tasks. The type of work might not have been very interesting for the 20-year-old, but the habits of his new colleagues were quite a surprise to him. Having been working there for only a matter of weeks, three other members of the L. Behrens und Söhne staff invited him to join a game of bridge. 'We played and drank beer until one o'clock, when I said I must go,' an exhausted Winton noted in his diary when he finally got home. He concluded about his new co-workers that 'as far as I can see we will not have much to do with each other' because Winton assumed they felt him too tame, and they – he rather unfairly described – were 'vulgar louts'.[14]

Winton achieved a more balanced social life at his lodgings. He had found a room with Herr and Frau Valk, whose house was a only twenty-five-minute tram ride from L. Behrens und Söhne's offices. One advantage to living with the Valks – apart from the convenience of his commute – was their very attractive maid, 18-year-old Gretschen. As they gravitated towards each other, Winton and Gretschen could often be found walking for hours together, talking intensely in German. Despite the fact that Winton was still writing regularly to Elizabeth, he grew closer and closer to Gretschen, although how close he never revealed.

Notwithstanding his feelings of being a misfit with his colleagues because of their drinking habits, Hamburg was certainly the making of Winton's social life. A shy man up to this point, he had always had a close but small friendship group. In Germany, he began to spread his wings and was soon the regular guest at dinners, and attended dances and theatre trips. The Germans were always extremely welcoming to Winton. In June 1929, he was invited to a dinner with two other men and three women at a newly acquainted friend's house. He was surprised to be asked to partake in a small Jewish ceremony before dinner, during which he did his best to pretend to know what he was supposed to do. It was not until they had awkwardly sat down for dinner that Winton discovered that everyone had assumed he was Jewish, so they had hurriedly put the ritual on to be hospitable. 'Apparently, they all thought I was Jewish,' Winton wrote with amusement in his diary, 'so I tactfully put them right.'[15]

A thriving social life and an attractive young lady living in the same house were certainly distractions, but this did not stop Winton from growing continually closer to Elizabeth, with whom he corresponded almost daily. Christmas 1929 was a joyous occasion for him as he was able to take two weeks away from work and return home to his family in London. He was immensely disappointed upon arrival, though, because, like ships in the night, he came to London on the day that Elizabeth left for a holiday in Paris. Nevertheless, it was a jubilant time for the Winton household. The evenings were spent in the company of good friends and extended family, with the usually shy eldest son of Rudolf and Babi having developed a much more outgoing personality to that of his younger self.

The intermediate period between Christmas and New Year, when time for most seems undefined, was an exciting one for Winton. The butterflies in his stomach were churning in the knowledge that Elizabeth was on her way back to London, having spent a week in the French capital.

In a romantic meeting on the station platform as Elizabeth's train screeched to a halt, they both needed a double take before recognising each other. The picture of Elizabeth that Winton had kept in Hamburg was of a girl and now he was looking at a woman – a change from a teenager to an adult within the space of six short months. They fell, respectfully, into each other's arms, Elizabeth's chaperone, Mr Sala, still gripping her hand tightly as she embraced Winton.

With only a matter of a few days to spend together before Winton needed to return to Germany to resume his work at L. Behrens und Söhne, the couple decided they would do something particularly special for the New Year. The Dragon was a private members' club tucked away in the back streets of the city, behind the London Coliseum. Towered over by the Renaissance theatre, Winton thought the venue was a perfect mixture of exclusivity and informality, known to house actors and actresses from the surrounding area. Unfortunately, Winton had not anticipated that his invitation to Elizabeth would extend also to her guardian, Mr Sala, who insisted on accompanying them. So, as they danced their way into 1930, Mr Sala sat glumly at a table sipping his tea and trying not to cause any of the arty types surrounding him to feel the need to strike up a conversation.

Before heading back to Hamburg, Winton and Elizabeth were able to meet once without Mr Sala in their shadow. However, after Winton left London – with sad farewells to all – the couple stopped writing to each other altogether. Whether or not they had agreed that their New Year's date was a way of ending their relationship on a happy note, from then on, there was never any mention of her in his diaries, and there is no evidence to suggest that they ever corresponded again.

Chapter 3

Rising from the Ashes

Two weeks away from Hamburg had felt like a lifetime for Winton. The seemingly thriving and exciting city he had left in December 1929 appeared completely different in January 1930. The impact on the economy was becoming increasingly evident: 'More and more people are being sacked in the office and the outlook is exceedingly black,' commented Winton in a letter to his mother upon his return to work.[1] Although this decline was something that had surrounded Winton during his whole time in Germany, he had been somewhat sheltered by the affluent company he kept.

L. Behrens und Söhne, like so many other German businesses, was almost entirely reliant on foreign capital, in a large part from America. The loans – used mostly for the massive debt Germany was paying for wartime reparations as part of the 1919 Treaty of Versailles – were instrumental in reviving the flailing economy. However, the 1929 New York Stock Exchange crash had grave consequences for German business and marked a point in history where things deteriorated rapidly for the German people.

Before Winton's eyes, the life he had built and loved in Hamburg was falling apart. The winter months at the start of 1930 were dire for him, with colleagues being laid off in groups becoming a weekly occurrence. With L. Behrens und Söhne now only half the size it had been when he had joined, what was becoming clear to Winton was that he would soon be following in the footsteps of his redundant colleagues.

On 22 April – jumping before he was pushed – Winton left the company and moved to the capital to find alternative work. With the help of his father's connections, he landed himself a more interesting, better-remunerated and less taxing job with a Berlin-based merchant bank called A.E. Wassermann. Having to move to another city meant leaving the friendships he had made, one of which was most acute. However, his emotions towards Gretschen had been clouded by his time with Elizabeth back in London, making his departure from his maid relatively painless.

Now lodging in the district of Mommsenstrasse, the young Englishman found himself in a comfortable bubble that was so far removed from the experiences of those around him who were struggling financially it felt almost fictional. While Winton enjoyed boat trips on Lake Wannsee and practised his fencing in local facilities, the lives of ordinary Berliners continued to spiral even further down into poverty. Figures from the time suggest that at the lowest point, one in three of the German population were homeless. Winton only remained in Germany for a few more months before moving away from this despair to Paris and then back to London, where he became a stockbroker, joining Crews & Company in 1937, where he specialised in arbitrage. At the time that he left Germany, there was a strange feeling of optimism in Berlin that an up-and-coming politician might be the answer to Germany's woes.

The name Adolf Hitler, leader of the National Socialist Party, was not one Winton was familiar with, certainly not in the context of politics. Twenty-years his senior, Hitler had already done a spell in prison for leading a failed coup, known as the Beer Hall Putsch. His five-year sentenced incarceration for treason in Landsberg Prison – 300 miles south of Winton's new home in Berlin – gave Hitler the platform he needed to spread his hatred. While in prison, fellow prisoner Rudolf Hess typed up Hitler's memoir as the blossoming Führer dictated his doctrine of animosity. Not quite rolling off the tongue, his self-titled *Four and a Half Years of Struggle Against Lies, Stupidity, and Cowardice* book was shortened to *Mein Kampf*, meaning 'my stuggle'. Claiming capitalism and communism as being of equal danger, Hitler ludicrously placed almost all the blame at the door of the Jews, who he believed were responsible for both.

Released after just nine months in prison, Hitler's newfound status led to large and passionate rallies themed around national pride, which soon started to catch the attention of the wider community. For the prosperous friends of Winton, Hitler's message was often dismissed as protest politics rather than something to take seriously. Despite this, every day more and more Germans started to like the idea of Hitler's ambition 'to create a racially pure living space' for the German people within a continent in which they were now at the bottom of the pecking order.[2]

Conceding 13 per cent of their territory and all overseas possessions, the Treaty of Versailles meant Germany was obliged to relinquish the Alsace-Lorraine region and the rich mines in the Saar Basin to France, return the cantons of Eupen and Malmedy to Belgium, whilst Denmark gained portions of North Schleswig following a referendum that went in their favour. Also, the city of Danzig was placed under the control of the League of Nations. West Prussia was handed over to the newly formed Polish state, which gave it much needed access to the sea, remedying its years as a struggling landlocked state.

Possibly most contentious of all was the Sudetenland, a slither of German land that split Czechoslovakia from Germany and Austria. Containing a wide variety of nationalities – mainly Czechs, Germans, Slovaks, Hungarians, Poles and Ruthenians – the area was incorporated into Czechoslovakia. From the viewpoint of many Europeans, with Winton not being an exception, these measures were tough on Germany, but fair given the huge destruction they had caused during the Great War.

For Hitler, however, rebelling against the confiscation of land was his master key to his vision for Europe and his manifesto for taking power. Claiming that native Germans living in this 13 per cent tract of confiscated territory – cut off from their homeland – were being persecuted by their new respective governments gave the aspiring leader an excuse to show aggression towards other countries. An article in the *Pall Mall Gazette* had pointed out the dangers of the treaty: 'Let it not be thought for a moment that the danger of another explosion in Europe is passed,' it said. 'The causes of war have in no way been removed; indeed, they are in some respects aggravated by the so-called peace treaties.'[3] The author of this article was at the time a maverick politician – Winston Churchill.

The speedy collapse of the German economy, witnessed by Winton, was followed swiftly by the downfall of the political system. The vacuum of power led to almost daily demonstrations, often ending in bloody clashes with the police. It was against this backdrop that the National Socialist Party – known as the Nazi Party – began to gain a countrywide footing, with promises to eradicate the economic problems by restoring the German Empire being received with glee. For the struggling German population, they knew that the land confiscated in 1919 was their most valuable, and without it, their economy was suffering. For Winton and his left-wing friends, the swell of nationalism across Europe, magnified by Hitler's meteoric rise, was incredibly worrying. A friend from his later life, Labour politician Alf Dubs, wrote in *The Guardian* that Winton's 'views were certainly to the left of the Labour Party and he had some scathing criticisms of the Labour government' under Prime Minister Ramsay MacDonald.[4]

The German election of 1932 saw the Nazi Party achieve a majority, with 37 per cent of the seats in the Bundesregierung, the German government. With this majority, Hitler decided that he would run for the presidency, unsuccessfully going against the 84-year-old incumbent, President Hindenburg, who won the run-off with 53 per cent of the vote. Despite Hitler losing the race to be president, his party remained a major player in the Bundesregierung, at which there was a stalemate without any party in a position to take power.

On 30 January 1933, to break the deadlock, President Hindenburg offered Hitler the post of chancellor. It seemed that for the first time in over fifteen years, the country had something to celebrate. Processions were rife around the country, with men, women and children marching the streets with candles, believing that this man would be their salvation from suffering.

Such was the desperation of the German people, the threat that Hitler posed was almost overlooked by the moderate citizen. He was well known for his hatred in his speeches and his writings. 'The stronger must dominate and not mate with the weaker,' he barked at Rudolf Hess while in prison, 'which would signify the sacrifice of its own higher nature.' Hess was frantically trying to keep up with this tirade, smacking the keys of his typewriter as Hitler continued: 'Only the born weakling can look upon this principle as cruel, and if he does so it is merely because he is of a feebler nature and narrower mind.'[5] Published in 1925, all the warning signs were evident in *Mein Kampf*, but were ignored.

Hitler did little to hide that, in his mind, the weaker of society were not limited to Jews but included disabled people, communists, homosexuals, degenerate artists, prostitutes, black people, intellectuals, philosophers, alcoholics, teachers, social democrats, Jehovah's Witnesses, gypsies, asocial people, Roman Catholics, Freemasons, those who were overweight, vagrants, drug addicts, open dissidents, pacifists and all non-Europeans. Not only were these members of society seen as feeble, but in Hitler's view, they were detestable, which he continually made clear as he rose in prominence. These types of people were, he believed, not welcome in his Aryan territory and therefore needed removing, by whatever means possible. Hitler would discriminate against all, with a merciless focus on Jews – well known to be Hitler's favourite hate group – resulting in one of the most horrific acts of human cruelty in recent history.

The Holocaust – the genocidal killing of over 6 million Jews, nearly a third of whom were children – raged across the Continent between 1941 and Germany's defeat in May 1945. With 9 million Jews living in Europe at the time, two thirds of the ethnicity's population would be wiped off the face of the Continent in just four years. From the outset, Hitler made no secret of his cruel intentions to persecute the Jews. Even as early as 1922, he was talking about eradicating the entire Jewish population:

> If I am ever really in power, the destruction of the Jews will be my first and most important job. As soon as I have power, I shall have gallows after gallows erected … then the Jews will be hanged one after another, and they will stay hanging until they stink. They will stay hanging as long as hygienically possible. As soon as they are untied, then the next group will follow and that will continue until the last Jew in Munich is exterminated. Exactly the same procedure will be followed in other cities until Germany is cleansed of the last Jew.[6]

But when Hitler came to power in 1933, his agenda focused on recouping land confiscated from the German Empire in 1919. His speeches, which were the main outpouring of his ideas reported by the British press, mainly concentrated on returning Germany back to prominence. In later life, Winton told politician friend Alf Dubs that 'he saw the impending tragedy' stemming from Hitler's popularity.[7]

Although he publicly declared that he would comply with the Treaty of Versailles, Hitler soon halted any further reparation payments from Germany. As the terms of the agreement on the territory of the Saar Basin expired in 1935, a referendum held on 13 January that year saw an overwhelming majority of more than 90 per cent vote in favour of re-joining Germany. The news sent shockwaves across Europe, with Winton commenting, 'I was very much aware of everything that was going on in Germany.'[8]

Hitler began one of his first propaganda campaigns, filming great rallies, which appeared in cinemas around the world. Although Winton was not one to be particularly gullible to right-wing hype, it was hard to avoid the rhetoric being released by the Nazi Party, and like so many others of his political persuasion, he was shocked by what he heard. At 11 am on 7 March 1936, three divisions of German troops entered the demilitarised zone of the Rhineland and swallowed it back into the German state. Although the locals wholeheartedly welcomed their invaders – for they had suffered far worse than those back in Germany from the economic downfall – Hitler ordered his men to retreat without a fight should other European countries try to drive them out. This was Hitler's chance to gauge the intentions of his neighbours to see if they would retaliate. Apart from some statements made by the French and British governments, as well as a condemnation by the League of Nations, the incident went unnoticed. Hitler got away with it.

Back in Britain, there were mutterings of Hitler's blatant violation of the treaty that his country had agreed to. However, only short articles from the inner pages of newspapers made reference to the events, with the *Gloucestershire Echo* dismissing any significance of the Nazi actions because 'everybody recognised it was bound to come sooner or later'.[9]

When Hitler next turned his focus to the 10 million Germans who lived under Austrian and Czechoslovakian control, the public started to take serious notice. On 12 March 1938, in what was to become known as the '*Anschluss*', Hitler's men marched into Austria. Although the previous five years had seen a gradual but brutal rise in discrimination and violence against Jews under the fist of the Third

Reich, the sound of jackboots goose-stepping into Austria beckoned in a new era of devastation for them. The subjugation of the Austrian Jews was instant and had hideous consequences. Just one day after occupation, all Jews in Austria were stripped of their civil rights and subjected to extreme levels of violence and humiliation.

Implementing the infamous Nuremberg Laws in Austria two months after taking control of the country, Hitler made little effort to disguise his intentions. The new rules forbade Jews from having a relationship with anyone other than a fellow Jew and instigated the boycott of all Jewish businesses. They also only allowed those with German or related blood to be classed as citizens. Winton was not a practising Jew, but this type of discrimination only added to his concerns. He recalled watching on 'with apprehension of the growing strength of the Nazis and the effect their propaganda was having on the people of Austria'.[10] What had started as sporadic attacks by Nazi supporters led to regular beatings of Jews by Hitler's storm troopers. Incited hatred continued, leading to the establishment of Dachau concentration camp in March 1933. This vast construction was the first of its kind and could accommodate up to 25,000 inmates. Nearly all those housed there would be Jewish.

The suffering was apparent all around the world, not least to Austria's European neighbours. With the 38 million casualties from the Great War at the forefront of their minds, adjacent powers were reluctant to offer any meaningful criticism to Austria's occupation. In fact, there was little protest whatsoever from the European stage. Appeasement was their only consideration. Even when the Austrian Chancellor, Kurt Schuschnigg, pleaded with the British and French governments to come to his country's aid, there was no action from either of them.

Winton was aghast at the lack of any significant response to the huge suffering that was happening so close to home. As well as the geographical significance, his family heritage and the time he had spent living in Europe made it particularly poignant. Although he did not believe in the use of military force, Winton was clear in his mind that the innocent citizens who were being persecuted by the Nazi regime needed to be the priority. 'I knew better what was happening on the Continent than most politicians,' Winton asserted in an interview in 2014, 'because my friends were all into left-wing politics and because of my then Jewish connections.'[11]

He was disappointed to hear politicians describe the *Anschluss* as an international affair for which they had no responsibility. The leaders of Britain and France claimed they did not act because neither had an official alliance with Austria nor an obligation to defend its freedom. In reality, they had their own problems to deal with, like the protests that dominated the streets of France as the government tried to grapple with their downward spiralling economy. In Britain, there were many strikes and civil unrest was rife.

By July 1938, the rise of anti-Semitic violence and the subsequent fleeing of Jews meant foreign powers could not ignore the situation any longer, leading to an emergency international conference in Evian, Switzerland. With government representatives from thirty-one countries present to discuss 'events which have drawn world attention to the plight of those whose presence is not desired in certain countries they have made their homes', Jewish civilians around the Continent held their breath for a solution to this spiritual discrimination.[12] Optimism was particularly high given the great turnout of representatives from so many democratic countries.

Sadly, no meaningful outcome was agreed. Just like with the Munich Conference, the European powers were so fearful of further bloodshed that the government officials present showed a complete reluctance to partake in any military action. With the concept of fighting aggression with military retaliation off the table, conversation turned to offering a place of refuge for the persecuted. In response to this idea, one by one, each government present in Evian began using their own domestic problems as an excuse as to why they could not increase their refugee quota. Britain quoted low employment levels and the post-Great War depression as reasons for the restriction of their borders. An anonymous conference member remarked at the close of proceedings how the word 'Evian' was simply 'naïve' spelled backwards. Until further notice, European Jews were on their own. Those who lived in the countries that bordered Germany were particularly concerned, even where they knew they had strong allies.

The nation that had possibly the most protection by Britain and France was Poland, which, a year later, following the launch of an invasion by Hitler on 1 September 1939, would be the country to give reason to force Britain back into war. Another neighbour of Germany that Britain and France were committed to protect was Czechoslovakia, a country of which Winton had a better understanding, thanks to his father's failed glass import business.

Czechoslovakia was founded by Tomáš Garrigue Masaryk after the collapse of the Austro-Hungarian Empire in 1918 and the Bohemian Kingdom officially ceased to exist. It was the only newly created state in Europe at the time to maintain its democracy in the years following the First World War, developing at a faster rate than those other states created from a post-war broken Europe. This was partly because the country was a multi-ethnic state, with half the population consisting of Czechs, nearly a quarter German, with the remainder including Slovaks, Hungarians, Poles and Rusyns. Part of the freshly formed Czechoslovakia was a region known as the Sudetenland – meaning 'the mountain region' – which had been confiscated from Germany after their surrender in 1918. Bordering Germany, Poland and what is today the Czech Republic, German settlements first appeared on this hilly region in the early thirteenth century. For hundreds of years, the German settlers lived peacefully alongside their Czech neighbours as their population gradually grew. By the turn of the twentieth century, more than 90 per cent of the 3.7 million-strong Sudetenland population were ethnic Germans.

However, the Sudeten Germans were treated with caution by the other ethnic groups in the country, not only because they were tarnished with the blame brush for the Great War, but were also seen as oppressors to the non-Germans within the Sudetenland. Therefore, resentment from the 3.3 million Germans towards the rest of Czechoslovakia began to boil over, especially as by 1938 and under Nazi control, many of them watched their fellow Germans prosper while they were still suffering extreme poverty and neglect. This was further magnified by the downturn in the region's main industries, in particular the production of porcelain and textiles, which had completely lost their export market due to the global depression. The likes of Rudolf Winton stopped ordering goods from the country altogether, there being no demand from his British customers.

Hitler took the standpoint that the Sudetenland had been stolen unnecessarily, declaring in an address to his party conference in 1938: 'the oppression of three and a half million Germans in Czechoslovakia must cease and the inalienable right to self-determination take its place.'[13]

There were divided feelings within the Sudetenland. The two opposing groups were the right-wing pro-Nazi Sudeten German Party (SdP) and the left-leaning anti-Nazi German Social Democratic Workers' Party in the Czechoslovak Republic, simply known as the Sudeten Social Democratic Party (SSD). Both parties had considerable support and often violently opposed each other.

Two weeks after the Nazis assumed control of Austria, Konrad Henlein, the leader of the SdP, travelled to Berlin for a prearranged appointment with Hitler. Although the 5½-foot politician with a large forehead and close-set eyes would not stand out in a crowd, he was an impressive leader, in the opinion of the Nazi leadership. He had grown the SdP from 100,000 members in 1935 to 1 million members two and half years later. While growth like this should not go uncredited, Henlein was in an advantageous position, given it was estimated that over 50 per cent of all Sudeten Germans were unemployed and therefore more likely to oppose their government. A closely guarded secret only known by a handful of people was that the SdP had been receiving unofficial funding from the Nazis since 1934 to finance their impressive campaigning.

On 28 March 1938, Hitler and Henlein met to discuss how the SdP – whose supporters accounted for over 15 per cent of the Sudeten German population – would be able to help the Nazis take control of the Sudetenland and incorporate it into the growing Third Reich.

Henlein returned to Czechoslovakia with a monthly allowance of 15,000 marks from Germany to fund the propaganda activities of the SdP – a large increase in the funding they had received for the previous four years. In return, Joachim von Ribbentrop, the newly appointed Reich Minister for Foreign Affairs in Germany, brought the SdP under his direct control. Ribbentrop instructed Henlein to demand the autonomy of the Sudetenland from the Czech President, Edvard Beneš, which he did with glee. Beneš, unwisely, did not take the ultimatum presented before him too seriously despite Nazi backing, as he was confident that his country's powerful allies were committed to securing their safety.

Setting his party members to work, Henlein led a campaign of unrest throughout the Sudetenland, putting unachievable demands on Beneš, known as the Karlsbader Programm. The more unreasonable the requests, Ribbentrop told Henlein, the more Nazi Germany would be willing to give him. The Czech government were only able to offer some token gestures to the SdP, which did little to suppress the uprising. Hitler made it clear that if these demands were not met, it would be taken as an act of aggression against German people. He therefore began to draw up Operation Grün, the plan to invade the Sudetenland, while Henlein pushed for a referendum to be held on

22 May 1938, giving the people the choice of whether to join the Third Reich.

Such was the hatred spewing from the Nazis that emotions boiled over on 13 September 1938 when members of the SdP started rioting in the streets. Beneš reacted in the only way possible, by sending troops to the region, declaring a state of martial law and implementing a curfew. It was only at this point that mainstream news agencies in Britain started reporting the problem. Although Winton knew the political situation better than did the average person, the escalating tensions in the Sudetenland took him by surprise. As the street fighting intensified over the next few days, Hitler publicly claimed that he had evidence that the Czechs had slaughtered 300,000 Germans in the Sudetenland over the last twenty years. Although this was widely dismissed at the time, European citizens were growing increasingly concerned that action was needed to restore peace to the area.

Desperate to avoid any bloodshed, British Prime Minster Neville Chamberlain flew to Berlin to discuss the situation directly with Hitler. Pictures of him boarding his aircraft filled the newspapers as the British people held their breath for a solution. Negotiations continued for several weeks, culminating in a meeting of several European leaders at the Munich Conference on 29 September 1938. Conversations continued into the early hours of the following day until they reached an agreement. Hitler got what he wanted, with the European leaders agreeing to allow a break in the terms of the Treaty of Versailles and give Germany control of the Sudetenland. Not included in the conference, Beneš had no say on this decision.

In return, the European leaders who were present sought assurance that this deal would ensure no further conflict. Neville Chamberlain infamously asked Hitler at this agreement to sign a peace treaty between Germany and the United Kingdom. Thus, the Sudetenland was used as a bargaining chip and was sacrificed for no meaningful reason.

Nevertheless, Chamberlain returned to Heston Aerodrome in Britain, where he delivered his notorious 'peace for our time' speech, stating that he and the German Führer and Chancellor regarded 'the Anglo-German Naval Agreement as symbolic of the desire of our two peoples never to go to war with one another again. ... this is the second time in our history that there has come back from Germany to Downing Street peace with honour.'[14]

Although historians have argued that Chamberlin was playing a clever game to buy Britain time to rearm, there were mixed reactions from the world stage to the Munich Agreement. Looking back on the appeasement, Winston Churchill stated: 'It is a mystery and tragedy of European history that a people capable of every heroic virtue, gifted, valiant, charming, as individuals, should repeatedly show such inveterate faults in almost every aspect of their governmental life.'[15] Even Russian dictator Joseph Stalin was perplexed by the outcomes of the Munich Conference, concluding that the West had actively colluded with Hitler, which, in some ways, they had. As for Nicholas Winton, he reflected many years later: 'Nobody that I knew at the time, who had thought that Hitler was a menace, thought that the crisis was over. I think we were just incredulous.'[16]

* * *

On 30 September 1938, the Sudetenland was officially swallowed up by the Third Reich. The Nazi-led SdP was now in power, and they wasted no time in focusing their hatred on anyone who had dared oppose them over the years, particularly terrorising members and supporters of the Sudeten Social Democrat Party. They were also openly complicit in Hitler's obsession with the obliteration of all European Jews.

The 1930 census showed that more than 350,000 people in Czechoslovakia identified themselves as Jewish by religion, spread between the provinces of Bohemia, Moravia and Slovakia, many of whom were German Jews living in the Sudetenland. Fearing for their safety, thousands of men, women and children fled across the border to seek refuge in what was left of Czechoslovakia after suffering the inevitable Nazi horror. An estimated 150,000 to 200,000 people left their homes and headed to Prague. This presented another dilemma for the capital's residents and the surrounding area. As many of those who fled were German-speaking Jews, the Czechs regarded them as symbolic of the enemy, so not only treated them with suspicion, but in most cases, as outcasts. A British official, who was present in Prague watching the situation unfold before his eyes, believed there was an 'unwillingness of the Government to retain within its shrunken borders men of German race [with] anti-Nazi opinions who are likely to be the cause of friction with the German Government'.[17] Logistically, there was also simply a lack of space to permanently house everyone, meaning about 20,000 people were having to make do with refugee camps that were being established around Prague, mostly in old schools, castles or village halls.

The three largest camps were Světlá Castle, Dolná Krupá Castle and Nížkov village school. Housing the most people, these makeshift shelters were incredibly overcrowded and conditions soon became uninhabitable, with no heating and a scarcity of food. As winter encroached, the refugees who now called these camps home had to struggle on without the basic amenities of coal, straw or blankets to keep warm. Charities from Britain were quick to report on the state of these establishments. Upon learning about them, Winton accurately commented that 'the conditions seemed pretty terrible'.[18] Little did he know that, within a matter of months, he would be a regular visitor to these encampments.

The government in Czechoslovakia were genuinely trying to help all they could, but the number of refugees pouring into Prague was unsustainable. Mayor Petr Zenkl had set up other camps outside the city with the Red Cross in an attempt to house the homeless. Nevertheless, the numbers were becoming too much for the authorities to handle, leading to troubling scenes of Jewish refugees from the Sudetenland being sent back in trains, coerced aboard by the sharp point of a Czech soldier's bayonet, only to be attacked by pro-Nazis upon their return. The Czech authorities claimed that they were concerned that housing German-speaking anti-Nazi people could 'serve as an excuse for further intervention and territorial demands from Berlin'.[19]

Because of this, most of the Jews and Sudeten Social Democrats from the fallen Sudetenland who arrived in the capital city drew the short straw and were only able to receive paltry hospitality from the state-built refugee camps. After just two months, pictures and videos of the appalling and deteriorating conditions these families were now enduring began to appear in the newspapers that were being read and newsreels being watched by Winton in Britain.

Mounting pressure placed on Prime Minister Neville Chamberlain's administration to try to assist the refugee calamity intensified, with critics of the government accusing them of causing the crisis – a condemnation that remains associated with Chamberlain to this day. Feeling the burden to take action, in October 1938 the British government allocated £4 million (worth £188 million in 2021) to aid those in danger from the Nazi Sudetenland takeover, with a further £10 million (worth £470 million in 2021) being loaned to the Czech government. In the statement, Chamberlain announced that 'the Chancellor of the Exchequer of the Government has addressed a letter to the Bank of England requesting the Bank provide the necessary credit ... and when the House resumes its sittings in November, Parliament will be asked to pass the necessary legislation'.[20] Of this money, £500,000 (worth £23 million in 2021) would be set aside to support the emigration of those deemed to be in particular danger.

Like many others, Lyn Smith, lecturer in Human Rights and International Relations at Webster University in Missouri, described this action as simply a way of 'assuaging British guilt after the way the Czechs had been sacrificed by the British and French'.[21]

Despite the view that things could not get worse, the events that unfolded on 9 November 1938 traumatised the world. Witnessed through the media, over 177 synagogues across Germany were burnt to the ground and 7,500 Jewish businesses were attacked and looted on what became known as the 'night of broken glass', or *Kristallnacht*. Far from intervening, German authorities stood back as the assault took place, later stepping in to arrest 30,000 Jewish men, who were then incarcerated in concentration camps, accused of inciting the violence. To replace all the broken glass from that night would have 'required purchase of half the entire annual production of the Belgian glass industry', commented historian A.J. Sherman.[22]

Winton had seen the warning signs from proceedings in Europe in the lead-up, but no one had anticipated the devastation that ensued. The shooting of German diplomat Ernst vom Rath in Paris two days earlier by a 17-year-old Jewish man, Herschel Grynszpan, had set off a shocking chain of events. Devastated after receiving a postcard from his family telling him they had been expelled from Germany, Grynszpan purchased a handgun and travelled to the German Embassy, where he carried out the assassination. Anger against Jews in Germany only intensified, resulting in the state-sanctioned violence on 9 November.

As the events unfolded, pressure mounted on Chamberlain and his government from the Council for German Jewry to relax the country's immigration policy, allowing free passage to Britain for the Europeans most in danger, which they eventually, begrudgingly, agreed to. It was certainly a generous gesture, which stood in contrast to the country's previous stance four months earlier at the Evian Conference.

Although the parameters were vague, the exercise proved advantageous for the endangered children. The rules roughly stated that those under the age of 17 were able to enter Britain from Germany and Austria, but only if they were deemed to be 'unsafe'. What was not specified was the number of those who would be allowed in or what circumstances qualified a child as 'unsafe'. The outcome of this was the creation of Operation *Kindertransport* (children's transport), or now known simply as *Kindertransport*. This was a merger of a section of the Central British Fund for World Jewish Relief, called the Refugee Children's Movement, and various other Jewish, Quaker and Christian groups.

With the anticipation that the suffering would soon escalate, the operation needed major funding, which came from the generosity of the British people, organised by former three-time British Prime Minister, Stanley Baldwin. Creating the Earl Baldwin Fund, he appealed to the country on 8 December 1938:

> for the victims who turn to England for help. For the first time in their long-troubled history, they have asked us in this way for financial aid ... the honour of our country is challenged, our Christian charity is challenged, and it is up to us to meet that challenge.[23]

His emotional appeal summed up the feeling across Britain, with citizens sharing his shame in trading the possibility of peace for the mass suffering of others.

Winton, along with thousands of others, filled the Earl Baldwin Fund with donations, rising quickly to more than £500,000. Of this, just under a half – £200,000 – was allocated to *Kindertransport*. From 3 December 1938, Jewish and other endangered children started to leave Austria and Germany. The migration continued until the day that Britain declared war on Germany, on 3 September 1939, by which time nearly 10,000 endangered children had been brought to the safety of Britain. Of these, more than 1,000 boys and girls would become old enough to enlist into the British Forces over the course of the war, and return to the occupied territories from which they had fled; thirty of them lost their lives fighting the Nazis.

Despite the £500,000 funding, the relaxing of border controls and the creation of *Kindertransport*, Winton was one of the few people in Britain to recognise that in 1938, the Czech refugees were receiving next to no attention in comparison to those from Austria and Germany. The British loan and donation to Czechoslovakia was only finalised and released in February 1939, over four months after the refugee camps in Prague were already bursting at the seams. As for the relaxed border controls, each immigrant needed over £50 to enter Britain, meaning that only the wealthy would be able to take advantage of the scheme, until the British donation was handed over. Finally, for some reason, there were groups who were getting hundreds of children out of Germany and Austria, but they had no support or interest in Czechoslovakia. The sad truth is that Czechoslovakia was not included within the remit of the *Kindertransport*. As Vera Gissing asked years after her journey to Britain: 'What about the threatened children from Czechoslovakia?'[24]

Winton was one of the few people to address this question.

Chapter 4

A Different Winter Holiday

'Hello,' Winton said, as he answered the ringing phone with some frustration in December 1938, causing him to drop the pile of knitted jumpers he had neatly folded for his suitcase onto the floor.

'It's Martin,' replied the voice on the other end of the line. A close friend of Winton, Martin Blake was a teacher at Westminster School (where one of his star pupils had been the charming, soon-to-be double agent Kim Philby, whom Blake was proud to see gain a scholarship to Trinity College, Cambridge). Their friendship had grown over the years, to the point that each New Year, the pair would enjoy a week's skiing together, courtesy of Westminster School, when Winton would accompany Blake as a helper for the school party. Even with the growing tensions in Europe, there was to be no interruption to this tradition in 1938, and the friends were due to leave for Switzerland that evening.

'I've cancelled the skiing trip,' Martin said abruptly. As Winton started to speak, Blake jumped in: 'Look, I haven't got a minute to talk to you on the phone, but I'm going out to Prague tomorrow, and I know what I'm doing will be of interest to you. Give up your winter sports holidays and come and join me.'[1] With that, the phone went dead.

This was surprising behaviour for Blake, who was as enthusiastic about skiing as anyone Winton knew. However, known for his strong left-leaning political beliefs, Martin had been watching furiously the events unfolding in Czechoslovakia, so Winton surmised it was perhaps inevitable that he would end up involved in one way or another.

With cautious intrigue, Winton switched his ski outfit for a thick woollen suit, repacked his bag and called the airline to change his plane ticket for the next available seat to Prague. At the time, he was not a man who would usually act on impulse, but he appreciated that for Blake to behave in the way he had – cancelling their longstanding traditional New Year's holiday at such short notice – it must be for something of the utmost importance. 'I knew he wouldn't say it unless he was convinced that it would be something that interested me,' Winton reflected.[2]

* * *

In the final hours of New Year's Eve 1938, as the British prepared to celebrate the arrival of 1939, Winton was touching down at Prague. He headed by taxi for Hotel Šroubek in Wenceslas Square, and checked in to room 171 to drop his luggage off before meeting Blake in his room. Blake had arrived the day before him.

'Martin was in bed,' Winton recalled, 'but not yet asleep. He told me about the refugees who had fled from the Sudetenland into Prague.'[3] After an hour perched on the end of his friend's bed, Winton retired to his own room for some sleep.

It was not until March 1998 that Winton made another visit to this hotel, now named Hotel Europa. On this trip, despite it being fifty-nine years since he was last there, Winton remarked that the room was almost exactly the same as it was before, saying, 'Yes, yes, I do recognise it!'[4] The suite, which to this day remains curiously similar, would become home for Winton over his three-week stay, as well as doubling up as an office. There were two rooms, one for sleeping and one for working. The rooms were well decorated, with fresh wallpaper, oak flooring and a sparsely laid-out mismatch of furniture. His return visit nearly six decades later showed that little work by the way of refreshing the room had taken place.

After a restless night and a quick breakfast, Winton met Martin in the reception area. The two men left the hotel, Winton following Blake as they navigated through the Czech crowds, all with hope in their eyes that the new year would bring better prospects for their country than the tensions of 1938. While walking, Blake explained how a group of British civilians had set up an organisation to help refugees escape the country, under the constant threat that the Nazis could arrive any day and arrest them all.

After about ten minutes of trudging through the freezing snow-filled streets, the two men came to a small side street, just past the National Theatre, where they entered the recently dedicated offices for all British-run rescue operations. Having to push past a vast number of poorly clothed, shivering and dishevelled cadaver-thin men, women and children lining the corridors, Winton and Blake came face to face with a young woman with dark brown hair and a look of stern determination, unlike anyone Winton had come across in his life. This was Doreen Warriner.

Three months earlier, just after midday on 13 October 1938, Doreen's 20-seater, twin-engine aircraft had touched down on the same runway that Winton had just landed on, at the brand-new Ruzyně Airport in Prague. Almost as glacial then as it was that day, the passengers aboard braced themselves for the smack of cold that would hit them when the door of the plane was opened. As a 34-year-old academic, Warriner was the only one amongst her fellow travellers to feel a surge of warmth despite the bitter chill. She was back in the country where she had spent so much time over the past ten years and whose people she respected and adored. But this time, she was here on a mission – a mission to help as many of the refugees in Prague as possible. Although many well-wishers were making their way to places such as Vienna and Prague to alleviate the suffering in any way they could, no one made as much impact as Warriner in Prague.

Born on 16 March 1904, Doreen Agnes Rosemary Julia Warriner grew up in a middle-class farming family in Warwickshire. Her father had begun his career as a land agent, before progressing into estate management roles and finally becoming a landowner in his own right. Her mother remained at home as the children grew up.

From a young age, Doreen was incredibly independent, culminating in her running the family farm as a teenager, having taken control from her father, whose failing health rendered him not fit enough for the task. Her ability to step up to a challenge, no matter the scale or her own situation at the time, was something she retained throughout her life. Her experience of running the farm from a young age also taught her how to manage her time well and solve problems quickly.

She attended Malvern Girls' College, in Great Malvern, Worcestershire. Describing itself as providing 'an inspirational climate which encourages risk-taking and sets high expectations', the school had a strong impact on its students, encouraging them not to follow the assumed path for girls at the time.[5] Like Winton, Warriner's schooling was hugely influential on her left-leaning political outlook.

Upon leaving the school, Warriner knew the direction in which she wanted her life to go. She was not interested in following in the footsteps of her mother by remaining at home to look after a family, nor did she did intend to follow her father into active farming. She wanted a career in academia, a highly competitive field and one that very few women had entered before her.

Warriner managed to secure herself a place at St Hugh's College, Oxford to read philosophy, politics and economics. True to her ideals, the college had been founded in 1886 by Elizabeth Wordsworth, the great-niece of poet William Wordsworth, and it was designed for less affluent female undergraduates. Several decades after Warriner's time at the college, it was attended by a young, politically minded woman called Theresa Brasier, who went on, as Theresa May, to become Prime Minister of the United Kingdom in 2016–19.

In her St Hugh's Day speech in 1928, College Principal Barbara Gwyer announced the 'pleasant success' of Warriner's election in the Mary Somerville Research Fellowship at Summerville College.[6] Gwyer was an impressive woman who ran the college from October 1924 to October 1945, seeing the place change dramatically in that time. Her calming demeanour was influential on all the women who passed through the college under her tenure.

Warriner thrived at university. Being surrounded by opinionated, bright and determined women was exactly the environment that inspired her. Her field of study – philosophy, politics and economics – suited perfectly her ethical and principled nature. The years flew by for Warriner and she passed with a First Class degree, quite an achievement for anyone, let alone a woman at that time. She went on to the London School of Economics as a research scholar, before returning to Oxford for the research fellowship at Somerville College. The rapid change of environment, from a small college she knew intimately to a university in the capital, did not faze her in the slightest.

Warriner devoted the majority of the 1930s to lecturing in Economics at University College London (UCL) and carrying out research assignments in Czechoslovakia. It was on these trips that she would not only learn the language, but also begin rubbing shoulders with influential figures, not least the country's Prime Minister, Milan Hodža. It was five years into her stint as a lecturer and researcher that she received news that she had been granted the opportunity to travel to the West Indies for a Rockefeller Fellowship.

In a similar impulse to Winton and Blake, while spending time deciding on the most appropriate wardrobe to pack for the Caribbean sun, the news of the refugee crisis in Prague – a place she had grown to love and where its people had welcomed her with open arms – nagged heavily on Warriner's mind. It was with seemingly little thought that she switched her one-piece swimsuit for her fur hat and changed her flight from the Pan American flying boat to the small land plane on which she had just arrived in Prague.

With no time to lose, Warriner headed straight to her accommodation in the renowned Wenceslas Square, aptly named after the patron saint of Bohemia. The hotel she checked into, the Alcron, was situated just south of the square on Štěpánská Street. Apart from her suitcase full of clothes and books, she had with her just over £450 in cash, donated by various people and groups in Britain, including £150 from the Save the Children Fund and £20 from the Royal Institute of International Affairs. She was there to offer her services, but what these services would be, she did not yet know. Warriner imagined something like the relief work she had heard about that went on in Vienna after the First World War, such as assisting in soup kitchens, cooking meals and handing out blankets.

But by the time Winton met her, Warriner had turned a barely existent operation into a major vehicle in managing the emigration of thousands of endangered Jews and Sudeten Germans out of Czechoslovakia to various places, most prominently, Britain.

Having been taken into Warriner's private office, Winton looked around at all the papers spread across every conceivable surface, while the walls were covered top to bottom in bookshelves, all lined with thick, dark-red, leather-bound books. She gestured for him to sit in a chair facing her desk, although he had to remove a handful of papers from the seat before being able to perch, somewhat uncomfortably, amongst the chaos. As Warriner dived headlong into conversation about the organisation, Winton was immediately awestruck by the extent of her passion and energy.

She explained in minute detail all she had achieved over the previous three months and how much there was still to do. As Winton enquired how she had got this far, Warriner reminisced about how it all started on the first day she had arrived in Prague, in October 1938, when she went to meet with a group of Quakers who had recently set up shop in the city. The group were intent on supporting the camps in a way that Warriner had envisaged, providing nourishment and some degree of temporary comfort in the cold. To her frustration, she discovered their relief work was yet to commence. Without any significant funds behind them, mixed with a lack of leadership, they had not been able to begin any work, and it seemed unlikely that this would change in the near future. The person in charge, Mary Penman, explained to Warriner that it was likely to be some weeks until they would need her assistance and it would be best for her to return at a later date. Having arrived in the country a few months earlier, Penman was a woman of significant influence as the sister of the Labour MP Philip Noel-Baker. Despite her status, she had not managed by this point to progress her cause by any meaningful degree.

Penman was acutely aware of the disappointment apparent in Warriner's face, so she told her about a group whose support for the refugee camps was more advanced, suggesting that she visit the man leading this work, Wenzel Jaksch. That same day, explained Warriner with noticeable excitement in her voice, she headed to Jaksch's flat on Hermannova Street. Knocking on the door, she thought that this could possibly turn out to be another dead end, as she was receiving no answer. After one last tap for good measure came the sound of locks turning and the door swung open. Standing in the doorway was a middle-aged man with dark, sweptback hair, a rectangular moustache and strikingly dark eyes. Nestled beneath his armpits was a set of wooden crutches, on which he leaned for support. A cosy looking tartan slipper encased his right foot, while his other foot stood squarely in a well-polished leather brogue shoe.

As Warriner launched into her introduction to the 38-year-old invalid in her best Czech, she was surprised when he answered her in English. She told him of her desire to help and of the trip to meet Mrs Penman, and that it had been her suggestion that she should come to see him. Despite having just met her, Jaksch happily invited her into the flat, which, he explained, had belonged to a friend and member of his party.

Jaksch, along with hundreds of thousands of others, had fled the Sudetenland as Hitler's men arrived. He was, however, in more danger than most, having recently been appointed chairman of the Sudeten Social Democrats, and being notorious for his vocally anti-Nazi speeches. Before he left his Sudeten home, arrest warrants had been issued with his name on them.

Although he had successfully reached Prague, evading the advancing Nazi soldiers, he was far from safe. For several months, Nazi agents had made their way into the city and were now grabbing people at will. Back in 1936, the Czech police reported, 2,900 suspects, 'allegedly acting for Germany or Hungary', were arrested.[7] But by 1938, the government in Prague was not powerful enough to put a stop to the ever-increasing number of agents now embedded in the country and was compelled to turn a blind eye. It was believed that if anyone was called for by Hitler, the Czech administration would happily hand them over to avoid conflict, and Jaksch knew it was only a matter of time before he was summonsed. Furthermore, no one in the country was naïve enough to believe that the Führer would not soon be extending the Nazi rule into the rest of Czechoslovakia. For Jaksch and his many supporters, it was inevitable that they would be either arrested in the free land or the free land would be occupied. All of this was a shocking revelation for Winton, as it started to dawn on him that he and Blake could themselves be in danger.

Over a cup of tea that afternoon, Jaksch had described to Warriner the predicament of his party, the SSD. He told her that he was committed to helping the whole group to leave Czechoslovakia together. He explained that to do this he had called in the assistance of some contacts, namely, the British Labour Party, the second largest political party in the United Kingdom at the time.

After finishing their drink and Jaksch staggering to his feet with the aid of his crutches, Warriner expressed her desire to help him. Jaksch told her that matters were now out of his hands, as the Labour Party had sent two individuals to run operations in Prague. Sensing her feeling of anti-climax, he suggested she come to a meeting the next day with these two politicians.

On the morning of 14 October, at the Grand Hôtel Steiner, Warriner waited eagerly for these mysterious men to arrive. Looking around the lobby of the 11-year-old hotel to see if Jaksch was lurking anywhere, she saw two men walking directly towards her who abruptly halted before introducing themselves as David Grenfell and William Gillies from the British Labour Party. Grenfell was a formidable character, with very short-cut brown hair and a thick moustache that looked like a shadow under his crooked nose. Coming from a poor Welsh family, he had joined his father in the coal mines from the age of 12. He moved abroad a few years later to work in mines in Canada, where he also studied at evening classes. After returning home in 1905, he eventually became an MP in 1922 for the Gower constituency in South Wales. He would go on to serve as Secretary for Mines at the Board of Trade under Winston Churchill's coalition government in 1940–5. Records show that Grenfell sat as a delegation member for the London Trade Council with Philip Noel-Baker, brother of Mary Penman from the Quaker Movement, although whether he made the connection is not known.

The other man, William Gillies, was a larger-than-life individual, with black hair slicked across his receding forehead, and gave Grenfell a run for his money with his moustache, which ran across his top lip and down past his lips to both sides of his chin, completely dominating his face. At the time, Gillies was International Secretary for the British

Labour Party and was feared for his incredible unreasonableness by all in the Houses of Parliament.

Jaksch had travelled to London at the start of the month to try to drum up support for travel permits for his party. To help his cause, he was able to use his relationship with Clement Attlee, the Labour Party leader and future Deputy Prime Minister during the Second World War, who would go on to replace Winston Churchill as Prime Minister in 1945. Attlee was able to introduce Jaksch to Gillies and Grenfell.

Although Warriner never recorded what was said in their first encounter, she explained that both Gillies and Grenfell were 'horribly rude and very difficult to get on with', which gave Winton an understanding of how this meeting unfolded.[8] Warriner said that despite their demeanour, she was willing to help Gillies and Grenfell. In turn, neither man was in a position to turn their moustache-framed noses up at such an offer.

Warriner described to Winton how these men went on to create the British Committee for Refugees from Czechoslovakia (BCRC), of which she was now the Prague representative, running all operations locally.

After this quick outline of the situation, Winton unhesitatingly agreed to do whatever he could to help. Delighted by this, Warriner set him up with a desk outside her office, where he was to support her secretary, Bill Barazetti, to meet and interview the queues of people wanting assistance. Like Winton and Blake, Barazetti was new to the BCRC – having only started working there a matter of days before – but stood out for his passion and willingness to take risks. Quite unlike the Englishmen, he had lived a very tough life, in part at the hands of the Nazis.

The son of a French professor at the University of Heidelberg, Barazetti was born on 29 July 1914 in Switzerland. Although he came from an affluent family, and clearly had close ties to influential

Czech officials – including the chief of police in Prague – there is next to nothing recorded of his early life. Winton believed that he was well educated, but never found out exactly what he had studied. Studying for a degree in law, philosophy or economics (it is not known which), he attended Hamburg University, where he was recruited by the Czech Secret Police. 'With my family connections and contacts, I was in a unique position to know better than most people what was happening with Hitler and what his plans might be,' Barazetti explained in an interview several years later.[9]

Barazetti described to Winton how, after graduating, he was sent to Germany to 'try to find out what Hitler's future plans might be'.[10] This rather general assignment – quoted from his obituary – is perhaps more embellishment than the reality. Nevertheless, once in Germany he set up a perfume factory, whilst at the same time feeding information back to the Czech police on the growth of the Nazi Party and the mounting hostility towards the Jews. Although there is no record to show the events that followed, it is safe to assume that at the very least, there was suspicion about Barazetti's clandestine activities, for surprisingly and suddenly, he fled Germany for the Polish border.

Once in Poland, he decided that he should return to his assignment, so he put on a disguise – dying his black hair blond and getting a fake passport – and was duly back at his factory, where his spying could resume. He recalled that at that time he went so far as to fake his own death, 'leaving [my] clothes on the banks of the River Elbe to give the impression that [I] had drowned'.[11]

Unfortunately, his hair dying was no match for the intelligence of the Gestapo, who quickly saw past his disguise, recognising him from the image of the man on the wanted poster, albeit with lighter features. After being arrested in the perfume factory, Barazetti was, according to the woman who would become his wife, 'taken to a remote forest, beaten and left for dead'.[12]

The details of the events leading up to this and those immediately following are sketchy, but apparently, one of the young girls working at the factory, who had taken a shine to the now blond Czech, followed the Gestapo attackers into the forest. There she had to watch from a distance as they beat him to within an inch of his life before going to his rescue after they had left. She recalled 'dragging him barely alive back to her village home' and nursed him back to health.[13] This would have been a tall order, as Barazetti was a well-set man, not to mention the Gestapo were not known for failing to fully execute people on their target list, and as a known spy, there is little doubt that his sentence would have been death. Nevertheless, there are several accounts from different parties of these events having taken place. In his obituary, Barazetti's saviour is given more light as 'an idealistic student from the Czech Sudetenland who was at that time sending photographs of Nazi training camps and of the burgeoning rash of labour camps by courier to the press in London'.[14]

While Barazetti was recovering, hidden in the spare room of a house, he began to grow close to the woman – called Anna – who had come to his rescue. Two years his senior, Anna shared many of Barazetti's anti-Nazi opinions and was, in her own way, acting as a spy in the hope of assisting in their downfall. The two fell in love, and Anna agreed to flee Germany with Barazetti to Prague once he was fit. The two were duly married in the Czech capital in 1936 and were granted a temporary Czech passport, albeit with Barazetti using a fake name, that of his great-grandfather, Le Monnier. It was at this time that the man who had once spied on behalf of the Czechs fell out of favour with his former employers for reasons unknown. This was brought to a spectacular head when he turned up one day at the Czech Intelligence Office – the company for whom he had nearly died while in service – to report a neighbour he suspected of spying for Germany. Far from taking his accusation seriously, the government body noted that 'Barazetti himself was considered unreliable' and they therefore did not carry out a proper investigation.[15]

Such was his fall from grace that Barazetti was unable to find gainful employment, so he decided to keep himself busy by volunteering for the Red Cross, while Anna was responsible for bringing in the necessary money to feed them and their newborn son, Nikolaus. While helping at the Red Cross, Barazetti was recommended to the BCRC, with his grasp of the German and Czech languages being regarded as particularly useful.

Barazetti and Winton got on well from the start, aided by the fact that both men were able to converse easily in German. While it is clear from their interaction that Barazetti genuinely liked Winton, his desire for friendship did have a hidden agenda. As a refugee himself and one who was known to the Nazis, Barazetti was, in part at least, working at the BCRC in the hope of securing a safe passage to England for himself, Anna and Nikolaus. A budding friendship with a man like Winton would only help his cause. Barazetti's role at the BCRC was that of general dogsbody but Warriner also used him to keep German spies out of their way. 'I used to know most of [the spies],' Barazetti said in an interview, 'big Nazis, small crooks and their innocent victims.'[16]

Winton wrote to his mother during the evening after his first meeting with Warriner: 'All the people who want to see Miss Warriner for information or help are asked to go any or every day [to be] met by Barbazetti [sic] and today me as well.' He went on to explain, 'Barbazetti [sic] is the secretary of Miss Warriner.'[17] During this first day, Winton was quick to notice the number of mothers who would turn up, desperate for some support, which the BCRC could only provide in the guise of small sums of money for much needed food and shelter. He told his mother about one woman who made a particular impression on him. 'She is going to have a baby next month and could not get money from anyone,' Winton recalled, because although 'she was Catholic, her husband was Jewish', so people were too afraid to help. 'We will do something for her,' he concluded, but knew that the small amount of financial aid they could give her would do little to help and would certainly not help her unborn child.[18]

By 5 pm on his first day, Winton was exhausted. He had met with what felt like hundreds of despairing people just like this heavily pregnant woman, and knew they represented only a small fraction of the overall problem. As he and Blake left the building, Doreen Warriner was still in her office and made little sign of being finished for the day. That evening, back in the beauty of Wenceslas Square, Winton was able to freshen up in the warmth and luxury of his Hotel Šroubek room before meeting Blake in the restaurant for dinner, where they discussed their first day in their new roles. As the two men mulled over the situation they were witnessing, Winton observed: 'The movement had already started – trying to get out of the country the adults who were in the greatest danger – but left one major problem unresolved: the children.'[19] Warriner was far from naïve of this point and had already raised it with Blake as a concern. Over dinner, the two men planned to set wheels in motion for what would be one of the most famous and celebrated humanitarian acts of the twentieth century. 'I thought I came to Prague well informed,' said Winton, but after just one day, he realised he might have been 'very badly informed'.[20]

* * *

By the next morning, Winton had made up his mind to dedicate himself exclusively to the children. With Blake, he presented the idea to Warriner as she arrived at her office. She was only too delighted to hand him full autonomy in running the newly formed and unofficial children's section of the BCRC. He recalled in a letter to his mother,

'Miss Warriner has already asked me to be Secretary of a Children's Committee for Czechoslovakia which I suggested should be formed.'[21]

Knowing he needed more time, Winton immediately wrote to Mr Hart, his boss at Crews & Company, to ask for an extension to his holiday by one week. Even prolonging his trip to three weeks would be an insufficient amount of time to organise something of this magnitude. He would also be without the support of Blake, who was due to return to England for the start of the spring term at school.

He voiced his concern to Warriner, who also wrote to Hart, asking for Winton to be allowed to remain in Prague for longer. The way she describes him and the language she uses in this letter shows the value she placed on Winton after having only known him for a relatively short amount of time:

> Mr Winton is, as you know, working with the refugee organisations here and has taken over the organisation of the child emigration. This is now at a very critical point and if he leaves at the moment, I am afraid the whole thing would come to a standstill. Could he not possibly remain [longer]? I am relying on him to organise the chaos which exists here and then to bring the documents to London. I am very shorthanded and have no one else who can take over the work he is doing. It really is essential if the plans are to go through ... [Winton's] energy is absolutely invaluable and he has drawn all the different organisations together in a most amazing way and brought order into the chaos.[22]

On 9 January, Winton received a rather abrupt letter back, stating that although his boss was aware of his 'heroic work for the thousands of poor devils who are suffering through no fault of their own', he would rather Winton returned to work after the agreed two weeks.[23] He made the point that money was to be made from the economic uncertainty in Europe and he needed his whole team assembled as soon as possible to maximise on this. Winton was disengaged and rebelled against his boss, and remained in Prague for a further ten days.

Now with only three weeks in which to operate, Winton had a Herculean task ahead of him, the scope of which can be appreciated from the daily letters he wrote to his mother. In these, he would ask all manner of questions: 'Could you go to the Immigration Section of the Home Office and find out what guarantees you need to bring a child into the country?'; 'If a family wishes to guarantee a child, what do they have to do?'; 'Can one get a child over if someone guarantees for a year? If not, can one guarantee for two years?'; 'What is the shortest guarantee required?' ...[24]

Winton's mother, Barbara, did not question her son's motives and immediately went about valiantly looking for answers regarding the legalities of bringing children to Britain. When all the material requested was provided a matter of days later, Winton wrote back to his mother: 'Thankyou [sic] very much for your letter ... the information was just what I wanted.'[25]

Outside of being able to settle children in Britain, the other issue on Winton's mind was the practicality of transporting large numbers of people out of Prague, across Europe and into Britain. Luckily, Warriner had extensive experience of this with the work she was already doing for the adults.

The first transport had taken place over two months before, led by the British politician David Grenfell. After darkness on the evening of 22 October 1938, he had boarded a train with fifty men in the hope of reaching Britain. Warriner had been present at the station, along with the wives and children of the men, to wave them off. After the train had disappeared from sight, Warriner and the women and children headed back through the cold streets to their dwellings, with no idea of the fate of their husbands.

It was not until another day had passed, on the evening of 24 October, that Warriner received a call from Grenfell to tell her their first mission had been a success. Travelling by slow night train, it took thirty hours for him and the fifty men to traverse the 300 miles to Poland, but they had arrived safely, albeit exhausted. Without any time to lose, Warriner was told to choose another twenty men and repeat the exercise, so as many refugees as possible could make a ferry crossing to Britain, a transport service that was already becoming less frequent. After a similar journey and linking up with Grenfell, Warriner was heading back to Prague to try to get another group. Two days after first leaving, travelling in five trains across three countries and with very little sleep, she arrived back in Prague only to do the same again. By the time that Winton had broached the topic of the children's transport, Warriner was a dab hand at the rescue operation and was able to provide much needed guidance.

These were the first of many such journeys on which the BCRC would embark during 1938. The exercise served as a blueprint for Winton to use in rescuing his children. He now had an idea of how they would get them out of the country and on to Britain, while his mother was busy working out the logistics of what would happen to them once they arrived.

The next concern was how to decide who should be eligible for the seats on the trains. This was where Warriner's expertise and – what some perceived to be a ruthless streak – was essential. She told Winton the most important thing she had learnt when she had first arrived in the city was to create lists. She explained to him that the key to any of the successful escape missions she had pioneered was to first understand who needed to escape, how many there were, and most importantly, who should get priority. 'I felt quite dazed,' admitted Winton. 'The size of the problem I had volunteered to help with started to emerge.'[26]

He therefore turned to the aid organisations who already had large numbers of endangered children on their books. There were five main groups with children on their lists: Jews, Catholics, communists, Austrians and political outcasts. Immediately after Winton had contacted them, each group understandably wanted the BCRC's newly formed children's section to prioritise their people. Winton asked them to provide as much detail as possible on the children they represented, with the very least, sending over a list of names to give him an idea of numbers. What bemused him was that all five groups responded in the same way, refusing to be the first to share such details, as they were convinced that Winton would send this on to one of their competitor organisations and therefore render them irrelevant. Such were the toxic politics that surrounded this humanitarian disaster that the organisations, who all had the same goal in mind, were now in a battle with each other rather than with their common enemy.

Winton used his business experience, applying an unsophisticated but clever strategy. He simply wrote to each organisation, telling them that he had 'a list from another group and would be using that unless they sent theirs immediately'.[27] This was complete fiction on Winton's part and he had no such document by this point. Nevertheless, within days the five organisations sent over the information he needed. Winton was now in possession of the particulars of 760 children. However, details ranged from full copy of a passport, school results and photographs, to merely a scribbled child's name that was barely legible. He therefore organised the list in order from the most detailed to the least. For those for whom he did not have enough suitable information, he would request more or even seek an audience with their parents. Using the Hotel Šroubek as the headquarters for the BCRC's children's section, families were told to report to room 171 as soon as they could to discuss the potential evacuation of their children.

Queues of dishevelled families became a regular feature along the corridor of Winton's hotel floor. Six-year-old Ben Abeles recalled how he and his mother 'stood in line on a winding staircase for hours until my turn came and I was registered. The parents exchanged their hopes and fears and we children eyed each other for potential friends.'[28] Despite the massive crowds, Winton would do his best to see each family individually, taking down details of their children, which included age and hobbies, and would have photographs taken if none were provided. On a daily basis, worried parents bombarded Winton with literally hundreds of questions, most usually asking, 'How long will it be before my child can go?' and 'Will I soon be able to follow my child?'[29]

Not only was this a draining and time-consuming activity, but the difficulty of the task was exacerbated by the fact that Winton knew hardly a word of Czech. He spoke German fluently, but as this was the language of the enemy, he found that people would refuse to engage in German conversation with him. As the nervous parents entered the office of the man they understood to be helping children to escape, they would become alarmed if spoken to in the language of their nemesis; many thought they were being tricked by Nazi agents. So began a rushed master class in basic Czech from Barazetti and others in Warriner's team. It is fair to say that Winton failed to grasp the basics of the language, and therefore settled on one phase in Czech: 'I am British, but I cannot speak Czech', which seemed to do the trick.[30]

The language barrier was not only an issue when communicating with those he was trying to assist. During his first week in the city, after what had been a busy day of meetings and visits, Winton went for an evening walk through the streets. His purpose was to organise his thoughts peacefully in private, when he stumbled upon a group of youths marching and chanting. For Winton, to counter the suffering he was witnessing on an hourly basis, any distraction was good enough, so he decided to join in with these individuals, with no clue as to what they were marching for and what they were chanting. As the procession of passionate protesters advanced towards the city centre, the energy levels increased, as did the volume of their chants. These men and women were repeatedly crying, '*Židé jsou naše neštěstí*'. Winton detected the tone of those around him become menacing as their faces slowly turned a darker shade of purple. He became alarmed as the shouts turned into full-blown screaming. Nevertheless, he tried to match the tempo and volume as best he could.

Suddenly, a punch was thrown as the protest descended into a violent scrap. As if they were expecting it, within what seemed like a second, the police arrived in force. What followed was a shouting match, with the police and protesters barking at each other like angry dogs. Winton decided that this was an opportune time for him to retire from his brief career as a protester, although he was still unaware what he was opposing or supporting. Back in his hotel, deciding on a nightcap at the bar to calm his adrenaline, he discovered from the barman that he had accidently just taken part in an anti-Jewish protest. The phase being chanted was 'The Jews are our misfortune', a well-known saying coined from *Der Stürmer*, the tabloid Nazi propaganda newspaper. Winton wrote to his mother that night, 'I must confess to having taken part in an anti-Jewish demonstration,' despite being of Jewish origin.[31]

Chapter 5

Sightseeing

Although the children's section was Winton's main work for the BCRC, he was always on hand to help with any other tasks. For instance, he would spend his evenings unashamedly networking to aid the BCRC's cause, as he told his mother in a letter on 14 January 1939: 'I try only to [spend each] evening with people who may be some use to me in this work.'[1] However, the main activity he was involved in outside his immediate remit with the children's section was to act as a sort of 'tour guide' of the refugee camps, which served as a way for the BCRC to highlight the urgency of their cause to anyone who would listen. For the Sudeten Social Democrat families orbiting the city centre, their makeshift camps they now called home were rapidly deteriorating from their already semi-habitable state. Not only were the living conditions unfit for animals, let alone humans, but this area also had some of the coldest winters to be experienced in Europe, meaning the inhabitants were only just able to survive the conditions. For Winton, such suffering right under his nose was hard to bear, especially as he felt the guilt of returning each evening to his warm, comfortable and safe hotel room.

It was agreed within the organisation that each time well-wishers presented themselves at the BCRC offices wanting to help by donating a tiny sum of money, enough to buy, say, a pint of milk, with the intention of heading home with a feeling of satisfaction, they would be offered a tour of the camps. Such was the suffering and squalor that confronted them, those who witnessed it first hand would mostly then dig deeper into their pockets to provide more funds for the relief.

One such visitor was Sir Harold Hales, a politician who had been the MP for Hanley in Staffordshire from 1931 to 1935, who arrived at the BCRC offices on 14 January 1939. He had actually already met Winton on the plane to Prague, having travelled there with the intention of selling motorcycles. Winton had gently explained that 'business might not be good under current conditions' and that he could better use his time philanthropically.[2] After a few days of unsuccessful vehicle sales, Hales took Winton's suggestion seriously and agreed to meet. Hales owned and ran a large shipping company called Hales Brothers, and in 1935 had inaugurated the Hales Trophy for the fastest transatlantic crossing. He was also one of the first recorded people to have crashed an airplane. His political career was even more colourful, with him often taking an unconventional approach such as passionately campaigning for the use of car horns being made illegal in Britain and debating the decline of the fishing industry in the House of Commons while gesturing with a dead herring in his left hand and his notes in his right. He had also been friends with the then recently deceased author Arnold Bennett, whose protagonist in the novel *The Card* was supposedly based on Hales.

After meeting Winton at his hotel, Hales was keen to see the camps for himself and was delighted he could join a tour with a sitting Member of Parliament who was also in the city at the same time. Eleanor Rathbone MP was an independent British politician who was one of a handful of colleagues who predicted the threat of Hitler and had campaigned against appeasement towards him since 1936. She was in the city to see for herself the impact of the Munich Agreement, which she had adamantly opposed in Parliament. She had also continually raised the question of the refugee crisis across Europe. Despite nearly entering her seventieth year, Rathbone was remarkably energetic for her age, and a formidable character with piercing eyes and grey hair tied up in a bun, who had no interest whatsoever in fashion. As Winton explained to his mother in a letter home, 'She never dressed, she just covered herself.'[3]

There was no doubt whatsoever that Rathbone was in Prague to provide weighty support, and being well connected to people of both considerable wealth and influence, she intended to exploit these relationships for the good of the refugees. Rathbone had conceived the idea for the Parliamentary Committee on Refugees (PCR), for which she was honorary secretary and David Grenfell was vice-chairman. She had called in help from her wide network of influential figures, leading a deputation of the National Council for Civil Liberties (NCCL) on 19 October 1938 to the Foreign Secretary, Lord Halifax, to promote the protection of the Sudeten Germans. Among this group was civil rights campaigner Ronald Kidd and H.G. Wells, the renowned author of the aptly named *War of the Worlds*.

Warriner chose Winton to escort Rathbone and Hales, as he was arguably the most polished among the BCRC. He was under strict instructions that the MPs were to be given the best possible treatment while not being shielded from any unpleasant sights, sounds or smells, which were now normal in the camps. He was also instructed to watch over Rathbone carefully as she was notoriously forgetful and would often misplace her belongings wherever she went, evident in a recent trip she had made to Bucharest, where, according to one of her companions, she somehow 'mislaid her coat and umbrella'.[4]

The intended smooth running of the tour did not quite materialise. Winton managed to lose Hales after only a few minutes in the first camp, so continued the tour with Rathbone alone for the next few hours. They eventually found Hales sitting alone on one of the makeshift beds, head in hands and crying like a baby. Despite being a very typically British stiff-upper-lipped gentleman of the time who had witnessed his fair share of atrocities throughout his time serving in Turkey during the First World War, the suffering in the camp was too much for him. After three hours, Winton decided that they had seen enough, so suggested they withdraw. He soon had to return to retrieve Rathbone's handbag, which had strayed from her grasp as they had been reunited with Hales, before retreating for a second time.

The day had been an emotional one for the politicians, but Winton recalled being 'impressed by the great interest [they] took in the condition of the refugees'.[5] On their return drive, Winton had a good conversation with them both, commenting in his next letter to his mother how they had held 'a meeting en-route back [to their hotels] re the reorganising of the children's section in London … [Rathbone] may be able to give us a hand with the children when she gets back to London.'[6]

The visit to the camps that day was not only influential for Rathbone and Hales but it seems that these two individuals had also had a sizable impact on Winton. That evening, Winton wrote to his mother with a greater understanding of the size of the task that lay ahead of him. He was clear in his letter that if he was going to be successful in rescuing the children, he would need to avoid the existing groups and committees that were also trying to help. This was off the back of Rathbone's advice, which was built on decades of witnessing organisations falling apart. There are countless examples from this time that show how, even with so many well-meaning individuals offering assistance, their bureaucracy, lack of organisation and in-fighting often made them more of a hindrance than a help.

This opinion was undoubtedly reinforced in part from witnessing the political tensions in which Warriner was now embroiled. She had needed to fight to keep her voluntary position as Prague Representative for the BCRC after she had decided to try her hand in public relations for the organisation. So frustrated by the lack of awareness of the dire situation by those back in London, she decided to act. She penned a long, passionate letter to the *Daily Telegraph*, which they published on 12 December 1938, and is extracted below:

> Sir – I want to call the attention of your readers to the urgency of the refugee situation here in Czechoslovakia ... Arrangements for direct relief to the camps through the Lord Mayor's Fund have been carried through with the maximum of inefficiency and delay ... The only way of helping these people is to find wider collective possibilities of emigration. Any other way is a palliative for one's own conscience only. In the last few days I have received several offers of cigarettes and chocolates for Christmas, including one from the Peace Pledge Union, which indicates that there is some confusion in Great Britain about the real state of affairs.[7]

To say that this letter caused some upset would be an understatement. William Gillies was enraged when he opened the right-wing newspaper that he detested only to read such a self-destructive letter. He quickly dashed off a telegram to Warriner demanding 'no more pronouncements', which she received with confusion. However, it was the chairman of the BCRC and seasoned politician Ewart Gladstone Culpin, who was also chairman of the London County Council, who wanted to sack her. He believed that such an aggressive letter aimed at contributors of the BCRC could cost them over £100,000 in grants from the Lord Mayor's Fund. He wrote to her saying how the letter had 'made much trouble' and followed with the chilling words every schoolchild of the time would have shivered at, 'I'll see you in my study', when she was in the UK on a pre-planned trip the following week.[8] She wrote in her diary that Culpin 'reprimanded me severely' but fell short of sacking her outright because, 'I had so far not received any payment for my work'.[9]

Despite this ordeal, upon her return to Prague Warriner did not restrain her outbursts of frustration about the leadership of the BCRC or any of the associated groups. Winton took her warnings seriously and was able to keep his distance to avoid the political aspects of what he was trying to achieve.

Even if he had wanted to, Winton's routine from the offset was so exhausting that it left little time for petty squabbling. Throughout the daytime, if he was not out visiting camps, he would be meeting and interviewing families, trying to gather as much data from them as possible. People began knocking on his hotel door from dawn, often before 6 am, and he would often answer with a white beard of shaving foam on his face. Everyone wanted to know whether they could get their children to safety, 'as though it only needed a magic carpet', Winton seared in a letter home, before reflecting, 'a magic carpet [is] by the way about what it does need at the moment.'[10] These visits would continue until late evening, when Winton would briefly freshen up before hitting the town to network.

By the time Winton had started the children's section of the BCRC, many parents reluctantly comprehended that it would be impossible for their whole family to escape, but did not accept the same for their children. They had to compromise by sending their children away, with a fading hope that they would be able to follow at some point in the future. Winton wrote to his mother that he knew that for the parents he had met, 'circumstances will prevent them ever seeing their child again'.[11] This was a heartbreaking prospect and one that Winton could only warn of gently.

By now, Winton had been in the country for ten days. In this short space of time, he had met hundreds of families wanting his help, visited various aid organisations, mastered a phrase of the local language and accidentally become an anti-Semitic protester. Warriner was very impressed by his work so far, writing to the BCRC leadership in London in a report that 'Winton is doing really splendid work for the children' in early January.[12] However, he had not witnessed any form of rescue, something Warriner had seen from the very start of her time in Prague and which had motivated her to achieve all she had.

Warriner had complete approbation and faith in Winton's ambition, drive and dedication, but feared he might become disengaged when he returned to London, so she organised for him to witness a rescue in person. Purely as a logistical aid, on 12 January 1939 Winton accompanied a group of twenty Jewish children to the airport who were about to embark on a flight to London. Photos of him with the children would go on to be shared worldwide many years later, in particular one picture of him holding a young boy, wrapped up from the cold, looking tearfully back to his parents. Other footage from that day shows the pure agony in the eyes of the parents saying farewell to their children, all without exception trying to force a comforting smile. After the children boarded the plane, Winton stood back with the sobbing parents and watched the aircraft build up speed and take off. As it disappeared into the clouds, he suspected that if any of the children could still see them below from the windows, it would be their last ever sighting of their parents.

The trip was being funded and organised by the Barbican Mission, whose primary purpose was to convert Jewish children to Christianity. Demonstrating the desperation of Jewish parents, they were willing to turn their children away from their own faith in order to guarantee their safety. The following day, the *New York Times* reported: 'The children will be brought up in London homes and in the Barbican Mission until they are eighteen years old, when, after training as artisans, they will be sent to British colonies and dominions.'[13]

In Winton's mind, this was Christian blackmail, used against vulnerable people who were simply looking to secure the safety of their children. His view on religion was simple:

> If you believe in God, then I do not understand what difference it makes if you believe as a Christian, a Jew, a Buddhist, or a Muslim. The fundamentals of all religions are basically the same: goodness, love, not to kill, and to look after your parents and

those close to you. I believe people should think less about the aspects of religion that divide them and more about what these beliefs have in common, which is ethics.[14]

In the months that followed, Winton would often come up against similar religious obstacles, but his response was never wavering, as evidenced in one of his wonderful mottos: 'NEVER SAY IT CAN'T BE DONE.'[15]

Chapter 6

Then There Were Three

Buoyed by the sight of twenty endangered children taken out of harm's way by the Barbican Mission, Winton continued to plan his great escape scheme. His time in Prague was running out, leaving a major problem as to how the children's section could continue without a dedicated person on the ground. Fortunately, it was in early January 1939 when two men arrived at the BCRC offices – in the same way as had Winton and Blake – offering to help. Trevor Chadwick, who was accompanied by a colleague, Geoff Phelps, arrived in Prague representing Forres School in Swanage, which was run by Chadwick's uncle. The school had sent the two of them over in an attempt to bring a couple of refugee children back to Britain to be looked after by the school for the duration.

The Winton story is not only of one young man's inability to watch suffering from the sidelines, but also of his talent in coercing others with a shared belief to also act. Winton's children's section developed through the contribution of so many people and important events, but possibly the most significant moment was when Chadwick walked into Doreen Warriner's office; this heralded the forming of the tripartite team that was to turn the plan into reality.

Given how significant he is to this story, it is important to understand a bit about what led Chadwick to Prague in the first place. Born on 22 April 1907, the third child in a family of four siblings, Chadwick knew little of his father, who had died just five years later after founding Swanage's Forres Prep School, which he ran up until his death in 1912. He was succeeded by his brother, the Reverend R.M. Chadwick.

Trevor's son, William, recalled how 'it was openly agreed by all members of the family that he became their mother's favourite and was horribly spoilt'.[1] As such, Trevor was the one chosen from amongst his siblings to attend the Dragon School, a private establishment in Oxford, founded in 1877 by a group of Oxford dons. As one of the top schools of its type in Britain, the Dragon continues to be known for its unconventional approach to education, based on the idea of children having an awareness and understanding of the world around them. This is evident in the recollections of an Old Dragon and former civil servant, Peter Bourne:

> The absence of rigid regimentation at the Dragon, being treated as mature beyond my years and being trusted early with significant tasks taught me self-sufficiency and the need to take responsibility for my own future from a young age. It also imbued me with tolerance and a liberal, open view of the world. I learned to appreciate the historic context into which my generation was born, giving me the strong self-confidence to believe I had been prepared to achieve anything I wished in life.[2]

This environment was perfect for Chadwick, who gained a similar set of life skills during his five years at the school. On leaving the Dragon, it was off to senior school in Cumbria, when he gained a scholarship to Sedbergh School, a Church of England establishment set on the boundary between the Yorkshire Dales and Lake District National Parks. At the age of 13, this was quite a move for him, from his previous base near his family home in Oxford to unfamiliar territory in another part of the country.

His time at Sedbergh School was enjoyable and fruitful, as he left with a place at Oxford University, where he spent his time captaining the college rugby team, betting on the horses and running up large bar bills (which were covered by his mother when necessary). It would be fair to say that his record of accomplishment leading up to gaining a scholarship and then a place at Oxford was not reflected by his achievements at the university. He graduated with a disappointing third-class degree in jurisprudence, the science, study and theory of law. However, it is clear that Chadwick's experiences imbued in him the belief that he could accomplish anything if he put his mind to it and alongside this, he had developed a craving for the unusual – something that was put to good use when he eventually arrived in Prague. Although he was very different to the straight-laced Winton, Chadwick's private school education had given him a similar outlook, which was perhaps the reason why they clicked so well when they met.

Chadwick left Oxford in 1928 and after contemplating following the family tradition of teaching at Forres, he decided on something a little less conventional. At this point, a family member described him as 'the black sheep of a conservative Christian family'.[3] With a flair for adventure, he joined the Colonial Service as a district officer and his first assignment sent him to Nigeria. The Colonial Service was a government-led initiative whose function was to manage the country's colonies, under the remit of the Secretary of State for the Colonies and the Colonial Office in Westminster. According to Nigeria's annual report in 1930 – around a year after Chadwick joined – the colony was larger than any other British dependency, excluding Tanganyika and India, at approximately 373,078 square miles (over three times the size of the United Kingdom) with a population of over 18 million. Although there were some incidents of violence, most notably the death of Assistant District Officer Barlow on 8 February 1930 caused by an attack from locals, the colony was stable, with production and exports thriving.[4]

The role of a district officer at that time was to act as the bridge between the colonial government and the people within the district, effectively acting as the local spokesman for both sides of the operation. (Chadwick would later find himself performing a similar activity in Prague with the BCRC.) This role, as a commissioned officer, would have promised him a rewarding career, if he played his cards right, with the prospect of becoming a colonial governor – the highest rank in the Colonial Service and of which there were only forty at the time.

His time as a district officer was a short one though, as he left after just eighteen months in Nigeria. It is likely that he resigned because he had fallen in love with a woman. Prior to his arrival in Nigeria, he had spent much of his time with his younger brother, Hugh, who was farming near Battle, the small parish town in East Sussex that was once the site of the Battle of Hastings. The farmer who employed Hugh had a beautiful daughter called Marjorie, who became somewhat of a fascination for Trevor. The assumption was that she was the reason for his frequent visits to the farm before he left for Nigeria, and in 1931, they were married.

Life as the wife of the district officer in Nigeria, which clearly had its dangers, was not as glamorous as it might have sounded. As the role involved lots of regional travel, it meant district officers' wives and families could often be left for weeks on their own – in a part of the world where they would not have friends to keep them company. Before the age of rapid communication, this meant that the yearning for home could be great and young wives might struggle with being away from their families. This was a concern for Trevor, and it seems that it was with little regret that he resigned from his role in Nigeria so as not to subject his wife to that lifestyle.

Upon his return with his wife to England, Chadwick fell back on the family business, and to their delight, he joined Forres School as a Latin teacher. However, the anticipation that he would settle down and enjoy his new job was not borne out. Trevor's uncle hoped that he would one day be suitable to take over the reins as headmaster, following his father's example, but it soon became apparent that he was not suitable for the task.

There were certain of his traits that were tolerated, even celebrated, by the school establishment, such as arriving at the parents' evening in fancy dress as an ice cream salesman and handing out ice creams to the children and their parents. Another time, he appeared in an afternoon Latin class with a completely shaved head, having sported a full head of hair earlier in the day, and with no explanation, he taught the lesson with no sign of embarrassment. But there were incidents of a less harmless nature that could not just be put down to eccentricity. Chadwick had become close friends with Bob Brown, the coxswain of the local lifeboat crew, who also happened to be the landlord at the nearby Black Swan pub. Unfortunately, alcohol became a factor in Chadwick's life, leading him to turn up late to class with a strong smell of whisky on his breath, straight from the pub or a fishing trip, and on several occasions, he did not turn up at all.

Despite all his shortcomings, Chadwick certainly had an abundance of kindness. He volunteered for the Swanage lifeboat crew, arranged for buses for locals to be able to attend sporting events and organised parties for less advantaged children. All this admirable benevolence would be eclipsed by the work he went on to do with the BCRC. However, during his time teaching at the school, the generous nature of his character came at a cost to those around him, particularly his wife. With so much time spent at the bar of the Black Swan, fishing with friends and supporting the local community, it left little time for him to be at home with her or opportunity to include her in his social calendar. For Marjorie, this was a miserable period, during which she felt completely alone. The very lifestyle that Chadwick had tried to avoid for her by leaving Nigeria was sadly becoming a reality in Britain. Marjorie later recalled: 'His life was pubbing ... his close friends were the local fishermen – he preferred that type, and they hero-worshiped him.'[5]

Nevertheless, they remained married for the eight years he was teaching at Forres, without any record of them separating at any point. It was towards the end of 1938 that news was starting to filter through the papers and radio of the persecution of Jews and others, following the rise of the Nazi Party. There were many stories of children escaping from Germany and Austria and coming to Britain for their safety.

At this time, appeals for sponsorship began to appear in news outlets, and the church networks in particular were busy in this regard. It is likely that Trevor's uncle and headmaster of Forres, the Reverend R.M. Chadwick, would have received such an appeal through his church. He decided that the school would be able to take two children; it is not certain why he specified that these children should come from Czechoslovakia rather than Austria or Germany, but that was his choice. He needed someone to go out there to help choose and escort the children back, and who better suited to the task than his adventurous and maverick nephew, Trevor?

* * *

Upon their arrival in Prague, Warriner interviewed Geoff Phelps and Trevor Chadwick. She described to them her journey to date and immediately introduced them to Winton, given his evolving role in looking after the children's side of the operation.

That evening, Phelps and Chadwick met with Winton in the Hotel Šroubek bar, where the men looked through the list of children that Winton had compiled. There is no record as to the criteria they were working to when they earmarked two boys, Willi Weigl and Peter Walder, to take back to Forres School. At the end of the meeting, they also decided to take a girl, Gerda Mayer, who was to be cared for by Chadwick's mother.

With the unenviable task of choosing which children to save complete, Winton offered the two men the customary tour of Prague's latest 'tourist attraction' – the refugee camps. As well as the thousands of desperate parents and children, the men saw for themselves the many lost and confused children without parents, some as young as 2 years old. 'We saw halls full of confused refugees and batches of lost children [and] we saw only the fringe of it all,' Chadwick recollected in an interview.[6] Like his recent tour with Rathbone and Hales, Winton immediately knew that Chadwick and Phelps were different. Writing later about this day, Chadwick recounted the realisation that saving three children was doing almost nothing to help the situation significantly. He mentally committed at that moment to try to do more. For most, the ability to save three children, give them a home and a new family, would have been enough, but not for Chadwick. As Winton drove them back from their visit to the camp, Chadwick offered his full services to the BCRC. 'I got a clear impression of the enormity of the task,' he recalled.[7] Few fully grasped the situation as quickly and concisely as he did.

Winton was delighted with the offer of help from Chadwick – a man who, although very different to him, had a similar sense of humour – and they pressed ahead with their mission with unwavering energy. 'Without dedicated and noble-minded people, which Trevor certainly was, our rescue efforts would never have succeeded,' recalled Winton.[8] The next day, Chadwick joined Winton in the task of meeting and interviewing families. It meant that the queues outside Winton's hotel room would be attended to more quickly, although Chadwick certainly was not as efficient as Winton. Having conducted hundreds of such sessions already, Winton was a dab hand at collecting the necessary information, explaining his intentions and answering questions in as concise a time as possible. Chadwick, on the other hand, would spend up to an hour with each family. A 9-year-old girl who was interviewed by Chadwick that day simply remembered that 'he was terribly charming', which put her at ease from the start.[9]

Although most of what they were doing was emotionally draining and tediously administrative – interviewing parents and children from dawn until dusk – an element of excitement came with being in Prague at such at time of unrest. For Winton, there was a continuous feeling of unease wherever he went, to the extent that, the day after Chadwick started working at the BCRC, while eating a sandwich lunch with Warriner, Winton told her in a somewhat embarrassed tone that he had a suspicion that he was being followed wherever he went.

'Of course you are being followed,' Warriner responded, as if it were the most obvious thing in the world. 'So am I and all my members of staff,' she added.[10]

After all, Warriner, Winton and all the members of the BCRC were working against the Nazis, who had agents all around Prague. Winton told his son many years later, 'It would be quite common to be sitting in the hotel restaurant and there would be two gentlemen sitting at a table nearby hiding behind newspapers.'[11] At this time, Winton was also befriended by an attractive woman who claimed to be the Prague representative of the Swedish Red Cross. The two met while Winton was working in the Hotel Šroubek restaurant, and they soon struck up a conversation. 'She was very beautiful,' a 105-year-old Winton recalled with a twinkle in his eye. 'I mean, it's traditional for a spy to be beautiful, isn't it? You can't have an ugly spy; it's a contradiction in terms!'[12]

Warriner warned Winton that he was probably being played, as she had heard from Barazetti that this woman was thought to be a Nazi spy. But when she started speaking about the opportunity to evacuate a group of children now on the BCRC's books to Sweden, Winton was willing to take the risk, especially after she suggested he should take her dancing. For several evenings, Winton unashamedly enjoyed the company of this woman.

The excitement of a potential romance did not distract from the task of collecting the details of endangered children. With the help of Chadwick, Winton had a comprehensive list of nearly 800 children. Each child now had a full resume of their background, interests and hobbies, several pictures taken from different angles and a list of desires from their parents, ranging from dietary preferences to exercise regimes.

However, Winton knew that this was just the beginning. He still needed to get agreement from the British authorities to allow the children into the country, secure homes for them when they arrived, and most critically, find a way for the children to make the journey. With Chadwick now as his partner in the operation, a plan was starting to form in his mind. 'As far as I can see, my work re the children is only just starting,' Winton told his mother in a letter. 'I shall very likely have to carry on in London.'[13]

When he broached the subject with Warriner, she was fully behind the scheme. She dashed off a letter to the honorary secretary of the BCRC in London, asking for committee approval to formalise Winton's role:

Dear Miss Layton,
Could I suggest that you put the organisation of the children refugees from Czechoslovakia in the hands of Winton? He is ideal for the job. He has enormous energy, business methods, knows the situation perfectly well here.

He has prepared the case sheets of several hundreds of the children ... and all that he needs now is authority to go ahead. It is an opportunity for the committee to get the services of a really first-class organiser.[14]

* * *

On 21 January 1939, Winton flew back to Britain with Phelps and Chadwick, along with the three children the teachers had been sent to collect. For Winton, this was a momentous time, for it was the first rescue he had masterminded, albeit in a much smaller way than he had envisaged. The journey enabled Winton and Chadwick to finalise their roles and responsibilities within the children's section. Winton would remain in London to deal with the bureaucratic and administrative side of the operation – allowing him to return to his job – while Chadwick decided to be the man on the ground back in Prague. Quite in character, and without warning, Chadwick took an extended leave of absence from his Latin teaching duties and offered himself to the cause. Winton was a little more cautious, opting to balance his job with his new extracurricular activity.

During their time together in London, Chadwick and Winton were busy visiting various charity organisations, including the Quakers and the Movement for the Care of Children from Germany (MCCG), both of which were doing brilliant work to evacuate children from Germany and Austria, finding guarantors and foster families throughout Britain.

The two men were able to convince the charities to expand their remit to take children from Czechoslovakia, given that as refugees they would have likely come from Germany in the first place. The Quakers already had a base in Prague, albeit without any real traction at that point, but the MCCG needed a bit more convincing. Both groups – already incredibly stretched – were adamant that they would only be able to take a small number of children into their care, emphasising that Winton and Chadwick would need to have another option for the majority of the nearly 800 children they had on their books. Probably a more important consideration for the men was that these charities were already putting into place the different puzzle pieces of bringing unaccompanied children into Britain, helping fill the gaps in the BCRC's knowledge.

From his flat on Willow Road, Hampstead, Winton assembled a team to help with his task. The team comprised three individuals: Martin Blake, Barbara Willis, and his mother, Barbara Winton. Willis was a young friend of Blake's who showed up unannounced one day at Winton's flat and offered to be his secretary, which was gratefully accepted. After his arrival back in London, Winton immediately returned to his office work, so he needed to think about how to juggle both aspects of his life. He was fortunate that his line of work had a tradition of finishing each day at 3.30 pm, which is when the London Stock Exchange would shut. 'I had half of the day to work on this project,' was his conclusion.[15]

While they set to work trying to arrange visas, transport and foster homes for nearly 800 children, Chadwick was high in the sky, heading back to Prague. 'Trevor then went to work and dealt with all the considerable problems at the Prague end,' Winton wrote in a letter years later.[16] Through negotiations with the various London-based charities, Winton agreed to find twenty children for quick rehomings by foster families already known to these organisations. This was a significant milestone for the BCRC, but it was not a long-term solution. Winton discovered through his negotiations that these groups had a very limited number of households on their books who could foster children. He recalled that by far 'the most difficult side of course was finding families to take the children'.[17] However, with some pre-existing relationships from the established charities, they were at least able to locate some suitable homes for what would be their first evacuation from Czechoslovakia. Chadwick had no problem in finding parents from their carefully constructed list to agree to their children flying to the safety of Britain. He personally accompanied the group of children on the twenty-seat airplane. The journey left a sizeable impact on him, which he later recalled:

I took my first air transport rather proudly. [The children] were all cheerfully sick, enticed by the little paper bags, except a baby of one who slept peacefully in my lap the whole time. The Customs Officers [in Britain] were a little puzzled and began to open some of the suitcases, which contained the kids' worldly treasures. But when I explained the position they were completely co-operative. Then there was the meeting with the guarantors – my baby was cooed over and hustled off, and the other nineteen were shyly summing up their new parents, faces alive with hope for the love they were obviously going to be given.[18]

Notwithstanding Chadwick's apparent success, he was far from positive as arrived back in Czechoslovakia. 'I felt depressed as I returned to Prague,' he recollected sadly. 'Only twenty!'[19]

Records of the time are contradictory, but according to accounts by both Chadwick and Warriner, the BCRC flew multiple planeloads of children back to Britain. Warriner recalled in her diary at around the same time how 'Winton began to get his children's transports going and flew off with planeloads of Jewish children'.[20] She had been keeping a list of those who were lost in Prague, their parents having apparently disappeared. Adamant that they should be amongst the first to get out of the country, her wish was granted when, at 8 am on Friday, 10 March, she watched a plane take off with these children, heading for Britain. 'Special plane with My children left,' she wrote in her diary that evening.[21] What is strange about this is that none of the recent accounts about Winton, nor any of the books written about him, mention these plane journeys, including the excellent biography written by his daughter. We know that several planes took children to Britain before the Nazis entered Czechoslovakia, including the one carrying the children whom Warriner had rounded up in late 1938. In a letter sent at the end of March, she wrote that it was through Winton's organisation and under the management of Chadwick that the plane was able to take the children to Britain. It is likely that this was, if not *the* last, one of the last planes to leave the country, as Chadwick recollected that 'on 15 March the air transports came to an end when the Nazis came in [to Prague]'.[22] There was also a plane that took twenty-five children to Sweden, accompanied by none other than the beautiful Swedish Red Cross worker who had seduced – or been seduced by – Winton. Whether she was a Nazi spy or not, Winton's gamble at allowing himself to get close to her had paid off.

The fact that these journeys do not appear in much of the literature about Winton does not mean that they did not happen, and indeed, we can assume that the families found by the charities that were already evacuating children from Germany and Austria did foster them.

Despite having some successful rescues to his name, a makeshift office in London and an effective team, Winton was acting on behalf of the BCRC with no authority to do so whatsoever. To get to this point, he had made approaches to the Home Office on behalf of the BCRC and even created headed paper that described his role as 'Secretary, Children's Section for the BCRC'. Thankfully, this was never questioned; it would not be until 24 May 1939, several months later, that Winton was given an official role in the organisation.

There is no documentation that details why it took so long for Winton to be appointed, although the delay was most probably down to the already overwhelming administrative burden on the charity. It could also have been that the BCRC did not feel it had capacity to help the children. This was apparent in a rather negative letter sent by the charity's secretary, Margaret Layton, to Winton, informing him that the children's movement from Germany and Austria would be unlikely to be of any assistance, and thus the British government would not support his efforts. The letter did not acknowledge that Winton and Chadwick had already flown several children out of Prague through this route. These were clearly elements of his work that the leaders of the BCRC were aware of, as the letter warned that the 'Home Office is always antagonised by a multiplication of applications' for refugee status.[23]

It was true that when Winton turned to the Baldwin Fund, they told him that, due to insufficient resources, they were unable to assist. Both the *Kindertransport* organisation and the broader BCRC were incredibly stretched at this time and were therefore reluctant to expand their remit further to cover Winton and Chadwick's work. As has been mentioned continually throughout this story, so many people were in need of help that organisations had to perform the difficult task of selecting the groups they were going to prioritise.

Without funding or support from other charities, the unofficial children's section of the BCRC was seemingly on its own. With this side of the operation falling to his remit, Winton needed to find his own solutions.

He did this in many ways, one of which was to publicly appeal to the British population's goodwill through the powers of the press. His ability to present the argument in a concise and persuasive way is apparent in the letters he wrote to national newspapers, such as this, published on 4 May 1939:

> Dear Sir,
> Tales of violence and war, treaties made and broken, concentration camps and social ostracism have become so commonplace in the daily papers that the average person has completely lost his normal moral standard. A few years ago the publication of a story about a number of refugees without nationality or home who were starving in No Man's Land, not being allowed admission by one country but being expelled by the other, would most certainly at the very least have made people stop and think. Now they are too inured to such tragedies to consider how they might be able to mitigate such suffering.[24]

Another report he issued to the press a few months earlier stated how 'it may not be generally known that by this time only 25 children have been brought out of Czechoslovakia' into Britain.[25] In this, he is referring to one of the planes he and Chadwick had enabled. Why he did not elaborate on the other journeys that had taken place thus far is unknown. Appeals also spread within the press, with letters by influential characters – coerced by Winton to lend their support – not least a member of the Unitarian General Assembly Council, Reverend Rosalind Lee, who had witnessed first hand the suffering. 'I have seen these children in Czechoslovakia and know the terrible state in which they exist, and the awful fate which awaits them unless they can be rescued,' she wrote in the *South Wales Evening Post* on 20 April 1939.[26]

With all the publicity now starting to pay off, Winton began scatter-gunning requests around the country, through adverts in the press, contacting large organisations and utilising his many contacts. He needed to find people who were willing to foster children for an undefined length of time. The responses were almost all non-committal, with one woman, for example, writing back to say, 'What's the big rush? Nothing bad will happen in Europe. Hitler will be satisfied with what he already had, and no harm will come to these children of yours.'[27]

Though this was a somewhat typical response, some members of the British public gradually started to agree, with individuals and families coming forward to offer their spare rooms. At this point, Winton noticed a pattern. He quickly found that people had specific requirements when it came to the child they were willing to foster. This surprised him and his team, as responses would come asking for just a boy or girl, sometimes requesting an age or even specific looks such as hair colour.

To deal with this, Winton had photo cards printed with six children on each. Not only would this mean that foster parents would have their own choice, but also Winton believed that sending pictures of children, with some details about their background, would help them to gain sponsorship, as it is harder to say no when one has seen what one is saying no to. He asked each foster parent to mark the child they wanted to sponsor with a large 'X', as if they were selecting a piece of furniture from a catalogue. The children's parents were encouraged to send anything they thought would help convince people to foster their child over others. Therefore, when a pack of photographs was sent to a potential sponsor, it was accompanied by a bundle of drawings, sketches, letters, or whatever else desperate parents thought might give their child the edge over others. Chadwick recalled how some demographics were more popular, with many guarantors 'stipulating girls seven–ten and if possible fair', whereas, 'boys of twelve and upwards were harder to place'.[28] This hard-line approach was the primary reason for author Matej Mináč to name his book about the rescue *Nicholas Winton's Lottery of Life*, in which he wrote:

> I thought how unjust life was and how senselessly cruel it can be … on some cards, two photographs were crossed out, on others three, on another only one, and there were many on which none of the photographs were crossed out. I knew very well that those children whose photographs were not crossed out had simply had bad luck … they had not been selected, and so they perished.[29]

Winton went further than sending these packs to people he thought might be able to help and writing to newspapers. He would spend his weekends going door to door with pictures, telling the unsuspecting inhabitants to 'make your selection there and then'.[30] It worked a treat, although Winton's son described this strategy in a lecture years later 'like going to a kennel and choosing a dog'.[31] Winton did not care how his tactics were perceived. He was clear in his mind that a child sponsored was a life saved and nothing should prohibit this.

As photo cards were returned to Winton's London address with a child chosen for fostering, his team would immediately cross them off their list and get a message to Chadwick in Prague, who would put them on standby so that they could leave within a matter of a few hours' notice. Winton's team then faced the task of accumulating all the necessary documentation for the Home Office in order to gain a visa. There was also a series of bureaucratic hurdles to be painstakingly navigated. A separate application for each child had to be submitted to officials, with an up-to-date medical certificate, and a £50 guarantee to be allocated to the individual to pay for the potential return of the child once hostilities ended or they became of age. A separate application was required for each child and eventually, after several weeks, an entry permit would be issued.

Far from ending here, the government rightly required information about the people who would be fostering the children. 'Strict personal references covering the guarantor's character and solvency were demanded,' remarked Chadwick.[32] Fortunately, this was a far more straightforward piece of administration, as the government had already implemented a strategy in anticipation for the evacuation of British children from major cities if war was declared. The £50 guarantee was a huge sum of money for the average British person, not least because the country had been so badly affected by economic recession. On top of this, of course, foster parents would need to bear the costs of feeding and maintaining another human being for what could potentially be several years.

Winton was able to gain support from various charity organisations to put up the money for the guarantee so that people who could not afford the £50 would still have the opportunity to foster a child. 'There was the famous musician Myra Hess [who] paid a lot of the £50 guarantee for the children and many other people did that,' Winton explained.[33] Funds from the BCRC and Winton's own pocket were used to cover the expense of the train tickets. This, in turn, was sent to

Prague, where Chadwick would then gain all the necessary approvals from the Czech side. For Winton, the money was never a big issue; the challenge was to find families who were willing to foster a child. Even with all the hurdles he needed to overcome, Winton was always incredibly generous in his view of the British authorities, saying 'there was no problem with the government at all', when questioned on the topic.[34]

In Prague, Chadwick's remit was continuing to expand. Not only was he running the children's section with Winton, but he was also providing essential help to the whole of the BCRC. For the children, each time he would receive notice from London that a child had been chosen for a new home across the sea, he would immediately contact the parents to inform them of the news. The parents were told to have their children ready to leave at any minute, while also being instructed on how much, or how little in this case, they were able to travel with.

Between Winton and Chadwick – and their respective helpers – a smooth-running and effective operation was taking shape. They had already evacuated several children by plane, although exact numbers in the early days of the rescue operation were never recorded. They were now putting the pieces in place for other transports, which could take over ten times the number of children as the planes, with their sights set on trains.

They had planned for almost all eventualities except one – what happens if Hitler's soldiers arrive in Prague before the children can get out? In early March, no one knew if it was a matter of days, weeks or months. But they knew it was only a matter of time.

Chapter 7

Occupation

In early March 1939, Father Tiso was being driven along the streets of Berlin. The Catholic priest had been collected from the airport by an escort of soldiers and was being thrown around in the back of the black staff car, which was being driven by a youthful and seemingly impatient man with short blond hair. Tiso was wearing his usual attire: black shirt and trousers, white clerical collar and a thick double-breasted overcoat, which barely buttoned up over his protruding gut.

He was not on his way to carry out Holy Orders – far from it, as Father Jozef Gašpar Tiso was the president of Slovakia, at this point still under the ultimate control of the Czech government. After the Munich Agreement, Tiso had taken advantage of the annexation of the Sudetenland by attempting to declare Slovakia as a free state. With this in mind, he was on his way to see the one man he felt could make his vision a reality. He was due to meet with the leader of the Third Reich, Adolf Hitler, and ask for his assistance. For Hitler, with the geographic advantage of bordering both Poland and the rest of Czechoslovakia, Slovakia offered the strategic foothold he needed. He was therefore only too happy to assist.

With the meeting having apparently gone well and now thinking he had the most powerful man in Europe on his side, Tiso returned from this secret meeting to Slovakia with optimism. Unfortunately for him, Czech Prime Minister Rudolf Beran had been tipped off about these treacherous talks. Summoned to see Beran immediately after his return, Tiso was given one chance to terminate all conversations with Berlin. Flatly refusing to turn away from his vision of Slovakia gaining its independence, Beran had no choice but to dismiss Tiso on 10 March.

This resulted in mass riots throughout Slovakia, orchestrated by the Ludaks, a group of the most extreme members of Tiso's loyal Slovak People's Party. The riots carried more significance than anyone expected – including Tiso and Hitler – as the Czech troops protecting Prague were sent over the border to Slovakia to implement martial law, leaving the Czech capital exposed.

The mood in Prague was growing ever more anxious by the day, so much so that on Saturday, 11 March, Warriner dashed a telegram to London saying, 'Situation very uncertain. Committee should prepare emergency plan.'[1] Back in Britain, the scenario in Europe was less apparent, and the leaders of the BCRC did not treat this telegram with the urgency that Warriner had intended. The next day – Sunday, 12 March – the people of Prague also began to relax a little as the prospect of the Nazi advance seemed to grind to a crawl, which turned out to be a typical Nazis tactic. They would call off the propaganda mission ahead of the military invasion. This was, metaphorically, the calm before the storm.

Four days later, Tiso declared Slovakia an independent state, and the Nazi war machine rolled into the country. Slovakia became its own republic, gaining protectorate status with Germany on 12 March, and ceased to be part of Czechoslovakia.

For Winton, this was a disaster for his children's section. It was by awful coincidence that that day was earmarked for their first ever train evacuation of unaccompanied children. The events of the previous week had meant Chadwick was unsure about sending the children away, but as the news began to die down, he felt more optimistic. Indeed, he told Winton that the train would be leaving on the evening of 12 March, and he should therefore expect the arrival in Liverpool Street station the next day.

The takeover of Slovakia changed this immediately, and he quickly dashed a telegram to Winton, saying, 'Transport postponed. Probably Tuesday.'[2] They rightly wanted to verify reports before sending children through Europe alone. The next day, Chadwick was satisfied and decided to push ahead with what would be the first of many unaccompanied child transports from Prague. This was the first and smallest trainload of infants to leave the Czech capital, but it had been kept to that size in order to test the reliability of this method of transport. With twenty in the party, it was also the same number of children who had already travelled over by plane.

On 14 March 1939, standing on the smoky and damp platform of Liverpool Street station were Nicholas and Barbara Winton, eagerly awaiting a very important arrival. They had been kept up to date with the progress of the train, a telegram addressed to Winton, signed by Warriner and Chadwick, simply saying 'Congratulations' after the train had left Czechoslovakia.[3]

The mother and son watched with anticipation as the huge green steam train pulled into the station and arrived at its final stop just as the sun was starting to rise. From one of the carriages emerged twenty exhausted looking children, all wrapped warmly in their coats and scarves. All twenty had a seemingly huge luggage label hanging around their young necks.

As Winton stepped forward to greet the children, the first he met was 13-year-old Karel Reisz, whose huge grin only just disguised the boy's mother's ploy of having the family gold melted down and used to replace Karel's teeth fillings, in case he came across hard times in Britain. Ushering Karel and his fellow passengers to one side, the final job for Winton at Liverpool Street was to ensure that each child was collected by their temporary family. The excitement and emotion of all those involved quickly disappeared as the children were whisked off to their new homes, leaving the Wintons alone on the platform. With

A familiar sight. The First World War broke out when Winton was 5 years old and he had to contend with nightly German Zeppelin raids on London. (*Everett Collection/Shutterstock.com*)

Rising to prominence. Hitler with members of his party in 1927. (*Everett Collection/shutterstock.com*)

The beautiful South Front at Stowe School, where Winton was educated. (*Fela Sanu/shutterstock.com*)

Tomáš Masaryk, the highly respected first President of Czechoslovakia. (*Everett Collection/shutterstock.com*)

President Masaryk participates in the St Wenceslas celebration in Prague during his second term in 1929. (*Roman Nerud/shutterstock.com*)

A massive crowd gathers for a rally at Nuremberg, Germany, in 1937. Winton moved back from Germany to Britain that year. (*Everett Collection/shutterstock.com*)

The start of the humanitarian crisis in Prague followed the occupation of the Sudetenland. This iconic image shows the emotions of one woman as German troops arrived. (*Everett Collection/shutterstock.com*)

Doreen Warriner (1904–72).

Trevor Chadwick (1907–79), about 1935.

Beatrice Wellington (1907–71).

Bill Barazetti (1914–2000), passport photo, 1937.

David Grenfell (1881–1968).

The rescue operation run by Winton was made even harder after Germany invaded Czechoslovakia in March 1939. Hitler held a victory parade in Prague the following day. (*Everett Collection/shutterstock.com*)

The magnificent Prague Castle at night. Winton spent three weeks in the city at the start of 1939. (*sma1050/shutterstock.com*)

Charles Bridge in central Prague. (*Hans Christianson/shutterstock.com*)

German soldiers invade Poland in September 1939, signalling the end of the children's evacuation from Prague. (*Everett Collection/shutterstock.com*)

Winton would send pictures of the children on his books to potential foster parents. This is the picture the parents of a boy provided. It is not known if he was saved. (*KUCO/shutterstock.com*)

After war was declared, Winton set up Air Raid Precaution centres in London. (*Simon J. Beer/ shutterstock.com*)

Winton later worked as a Red Cross ambulance driver, transporting victims from nightly bombing raids on Britain. (*Everett Collection/shutterstock.com*)

Dead bodies of the men of Lidice, executed by the Nazis in retaliation for the assassination of Reinhard Heydrich. (*Everett Collection/shutterstock.com*)

The crematorium in Auschwitz, where up to 1.3 million people are thought to have been killed. (*agsaz/shutterstock.com*)

It was only after the Allied victory that the true scale of the atrocities of the Third Reich came to light. Liberated prisoners are taken to hospital in May 1945. (*Everett Collection/shutterstock.com*)

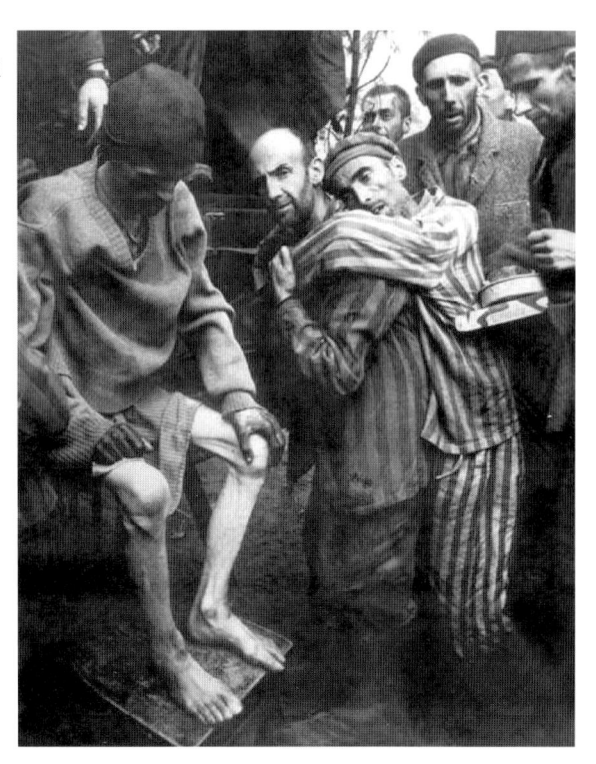

After the war, Winton worked for the Director of Reparations, dealing with materials stolen by the Nazis. Items included gold teeth and fillings, children's toys and wedding rings. (*Everett Collection/shutterstock.com*)

The truth about Winton's humanitarian work only came to light in the 1980s. A statue of Winton was erected in Wilson Station in Prague. (*Anton Kudelin/shutterstock.com*)

Later, a statue was placed in Maidenhead of Winton looking through his scrapbook. (*CarlsPix/shutterstock.com*)

Winton, aged 102, receiving an award in Prague. He lived to the remarkable age of 106. (*Michal Kalasek/shutterstock.com*)

The Winton family have continued to campaign for child refugees. Here, Nicholas's daughter Barbara Winton is speaking at a demonstration in 2019. (*Jonathan Tallon/shutterstock*)

his mother heading back to Willow Road to continue her committee work, Winton had to contemplate a day in the Stock Exchange.

The first trainload of children arriving in London provided a huge boost of confidence for everyone involved in the operation in Prague. Warriner was delighted, writing to Winton on 16 March 1939:

British Committee for Refugees from Czechoslovakia

Dear Nicky

I do congratulate you most sincerely in this great achievement, and know what an effort it must have been. I am so glad the sword never rested in your hand. I am going to ask Chadwick to organise the [next group of] children. There are a great number of things I want to write about, but the chief thing is to congratulate you and I must wait till times are quieter; today is a bad time ...

Yours,
Doreen

Not only did this mark a hugely successful moment, it was also the point at which Winton and Chadwick realised that the list of 800 children they had compiled months before might actually be a realistic target. But a monumental amount of work was required to achieve this.

At the same time that the children were being greeted at Liverpool Street on 14 March, Warriner was only just beginning to drift off to sleep after a frantic night with her thoughts racing around in her head. Just as her concentration was ebbing and sleep was setting in, the telephone rang. It was Douglas Reed, a volunteer from her office, informing her that the Nazis had now crossed the frontier and were making their way to Prague. They had met no resistance and there was nothing that would slow them down. Reed told her that it was now a matter of hours before the jackboots would be sounding down the streets of the Czech capital. Under these circumstances, Warriner's comment to Winton that 'today is a bad time' seems nothing short of an extreme understatement.

The BCRC was prepared more than most for such an eventuality because of a very useful contact. Warriner had become friendly with the passport control officer in the British Legation, a man named Harold Gibson, known to his superiors as Gibby. Warriner remembered him as 'a small, slight figure with a moustache in proportion'.[4] She later wrote that the passport official was 'always fully informed' and therefore his information should always be treated with the utmost urgency. It turned out that the reason Gibson was such a reliable source was because, unbeknown to Warriner, he worked for the British Secret Intelligence Service (SIS), commonly known as MI6. Like so many, he is an unsung hero in this story, for his warnings of an imminent invasion were far more accurate than the rumours spinning around the city. According to a friend of Winton's, he had 'allowed them to see a map that illustrated how Germany planned to occupy the rest of Europe'.[5]

By midday, the Nazis had arrived. The city from which so many people had fled to safety was now Hitler's latest conquest. The country that represented the liberty from the German oppression after the 1914 to 1918 war was no longer free, or safe. Being one of the more luxurious hotels in Prague, Warriner's temporary home at the Alcron was now filled with the most senior Nazi officers, all trying to earmark rooms for themselves. Only a few hours before this, Warriner had left through the empty lobby of a fairly quiet building in an attempt to help wanted individuals evade the Nazis. That same day, just a few hours later, she was walking through the same building, which had now become the nerve centre of the people she had been so desperately opposing.

As darkness descended on the city, with a new curfew being reluctantly respected, the streets of Prague were deserted; the invading vehicles and soldiers had also quietened down. The city had gone through a transformation that day, to the extent that it seemed like a completely different place to the one where Winton had spent three weeks only a month before.

For Warriner, that day was a blur, travelling between her office, the hotel and the British Legation, which is where she found herself after the curfew. It would be too late and too dangerous for her to make her own way back to her hotel. She gratefully accepted an invitation to stay in one of the Legation rooms. On the top floor, from her bedroom window she could see Prague Castle, brightly lit as usual, only now showing giant swastika flags hanging down. Unbeknown to Warriner, inside slept the most dangerous man in the world – Adolf Hitler. He had come to the city that night in order to take part in a hastily arranged victory parade through the streets. Rumour has it that he saw the ghost of the Czech founding president, Tomáš Masaryk, an experience that apparently had such an effect on the Führer that he was unable to sleep for the rest of the night. Warriner confessed that she felt a sense of glee when she heard of this tale, years later.

Two days after the invasion, Thursday, 16 March was earmarked for Hitler's victory parade through Prague, meaning the city was in gridlock, with Wenceslas Square completely shut off to its residents. Hitler had not come to the city alone, as his arrival had coincided with that of the dreaded Gestapo. As part of the SS and led by the Chief of German Police Heinrich Himmler, the Gestapo was the 32,000-strong German Secret Police. Sent to lead Gestapo operations in Prague was Kriminalrat Karl Bömelburg, a 54-year-old 'elderly, smiling gentleman, far from sinister', as Chadwick later reflected.[6] Bömelburg reached Czechoslovakia following an assignment in Paris to investigate the assassination of German diplomat Ernst vom Rath in 1938. The killing, carried out by Polish-German Jew

Herschel Grynszpan, was a particularly high-profile case, especially as *Kristallnacht* took place only hours after the attack. Bömelburg was chosen for this assignment partly on merit, but more so because he had lived as a child in France for five years and spoke the language well. He arrived in Prague under a bit of cloud after having been expelled from Paris, accused of helping far-right extremists and Nazi sympathisers.

Winton's recollection from London of this time was that 'all our activities quickly and secretly [needed to] take place behind the backs of the German Gestapo'.[7] This was not strictly true, as Chadwick had wasted no time in trying to introduce himself to Kriminalrat Bömelburg, with whom he hoped 'to negotiate with for the issue of exit permits for the children'.[8] He was able to arrange an introduction through a British official called Robert Stopford, with whom Warriner was working closely. Winton was full of admiration for the way that Chadwick threw himself into the task: 'He continued to carry on even when it became more difficult and dangerous when the Germans arrived.'[9]

From their first meeting, the relationship Chadwick built up with Bömelburg was essential to the continued success of the children's transports. The Gestapo chief became known as 'the criminal rat' to Chadwick, due to his unfortunate title. Chadwick wrote in a letter, years later, 'I remember my deep delight in the word Kriminalrat.'[10] The Kriminalrat was a mid-level police rank used within the SD as the equivalent to the rank of superintendent in a normal policing organisation. Typically responsible for gathering intelligence on political opponents and individuals deemed to be threats to the Nazi regime, the rank was usually given to people who had been at the level for less than three years.

For Chadwick, it is a true testament to his character that he was able to secure the trust and respect of the Germans so quickly. He recollected how he had to fight his way into gaining Bömelburg's confidence as his deputies 'gave me an unpleasant time at first and I remember putting on the screaming table-thumping act – always reliable with those louts – and demanding an interview with the Kriminalrat', which he was eventually granted.[11] From then on, 'he [Bömelburg] made things easier for me' and somewhat naïvely enabled many children to escape.[12] Chadwick's courage and bravery in being so direct with the Gestapo, a feared and deadly group, should not be underestimated. In his typical self-effacing style, he did not speak of his achievements and apparently kept even Winton in the dark. He never divulged why this was, but if it was because Chadwick had been frightened, he made a very good job of hiding it. He described the lethal Gestapo chief as 'an elderly, smiling gentleman, far from sinister, who eventually proved to be a great help'.[13] It is strange that Winton seemed not to be able to recollect any such relationship, which clearly was there, as attested to by Warriner and several British officials in Prague.

Despite the rapport built by Chadwick, the Gestapo would occasionally prove to be somewhat of a nuisance at times, particularly as on the day they arrived in Prague, they took over the BCRC offices, leaving the team to work from wherever they could, including the British Legation and the volunteers' hotel rooms. During one of his first meetings with the Gestapo chief, the topic of Warriner's former office was mentioned to Chadwick. Bömelburg stated how disappointed and surprised he had been with what they had found, claiming that although it was suspected that her work had been underhand, they were shocked and confused by her untoward activities. Chadwick was becoming increasingly worried that Warriner had left details of some of the underground and illegal work with which she was involved in hiding wanted people and enabling them to evade the Nazis.

In fact, they had found something much more peculiar. Pornography. And lots of it. There were bookshelves all around Warriner's office, filled with thick, red, leather-bound books containing hard-core German pornography. The building that the BCRC had requisitioned for their headquarters used to belong to a publishing company who had a line in post-First World War erotic photography. Warriner had adopted one of their storerooms as an office, which happened to be lined with a lot of back stock. She had asked for their removal on several occasions, but given the level of activity, this soon fell to the bottom of the priority list. The Nazi officers who had made the discovery took all the books away for thorough examination, apparently needing to check the content of each book in private – ostensibly one of their more enjoyable tasks that winter.

Although this was a light-hearted interaction between the Gestapo and the BCRC, it served as a distraction to what was really going on. The metaphorical noose was tightening around Warriner's neck and it would only be a matter of time before she was arrested. Some of her team had already succumbed to such a fate, with one Canadian woman working for the BCRC detained under the belief she was Warriner. The Nazi stance remained that if the BCRC were removing Jews from the Third Reich, they were serving an effective purpose. However, they were now convinced that the organisation was a front for anti-Nazis to evade arrest. The only way for the BCRC to continue would be to place the blame for any clandestine activity solely on Warriner's shoulders. She became the scapegoat, deemed to have been responsible for much of the illegal activity – saving the lives of some of the most wanted people in the country. The reasons for her ousting were not completely unfounded. Reluctantly, she accepted that for the good of those she was trying to help, she needed to hand over the reins to others, and left the country on 23 April 1939.

Thanks to his blossoming relationship with Bömelburg, Chadwick was asked to take on a bigger role within the BCRC, filling some of the void left by Warriner. Now responsible for relations with the Nazis, his first commitment remained the children's section. From the start of 1939, after Winton had returned to London to manage that end of the operation, Chadwick had been adding names to the list of 800 people compiled by Winton. One child recalled her meeting with Chadwick – who was now operating out of a makeshift office in his hotel suite – when he interviewed her for a place on his list:

> It took place in the Alcron, Prague's best hotel. We had all dressed very neatly for the occasion, my father in a formal suit. Trevor Chadwick, tall, handsome, with strikingly Nordic looks, descended the stairs, dressed in an old fisherman's jersey! He was terribly charming.[14]

Within the space of two months of having been in the country, Chadwick had added over 5,000 names of children to the BCRC's existing list of 800, all wanting asylum in Britain. Each evening, more names were sent by telegram to Winton's home, where they would be added to a ledger. Each time Winton wrote to a news outlet, he provided an updated number of children in need of a home. In the summer of 1939, the *Newcastle Evening Chronicle* reported that 'Mr Nicholas Winton said he had 6,000 children on his books waiting to be brought to this country'.[15] Chadwick was less clear about the number of children, 'but it must have been in the thousands', he remembered.[16] By this time, they had only managed to arrange for 2 per cent of them to leave the country – five planeloads of twenty children and one trainload of a further twenty – and the enormity of what was still to come caused them no end of concern. Chadwick also could not recall how many children had got away by this point, 'but it was only hundreds, alas'.[17]

Nevertheless, Chadwick and Winton worked tirelessly to arrange for the next transport to leave. They were not able to operate at the same speed as Warriner had with the adult section, as the new strict measures the occupying Nazis had implemented meant that their procedures were even more tedious and time-consuming. It was testament to Chadwick in particular, who had to navigate the very challenging and tense situation in Prague. Winton recalled that it was at this point that 'I knew Chadwick was the right man for the job', complimenting him for working 'like a beaver, and when the Germans entered Prague in March he remained there and carried on under great difficulties'.[18] Like Winton, Chadwick had originally worked out of his hotel room, but as the size of his operation grew, he found some office space belonging to a member of the Czech Cabinet in the heart of Prague's financial district, on Voršilská Street, where he had two members of staff working for him. It was on Voršilská Street that the children's section grew into an operation that evacuated hundreds of children rather than just tens.

Chapter 8

23:00 from Wilson Station

As the month of April began, despite the repeated interference from the Gestapo, Winton and Chadwick were nearly ready for their second trainload to leave Prague. The departure, like on the first train of twenty children, took place at 7.30 pm on 18 April from Wilson Station, named after American President Woodrow Wilson. By this time, the moonlight was making its way through the front of the huge stained glass semi-circular windows towering over the front entrance, casting its radiance on the German soldiers, who were now a regular feature swarming across the station on patrol. Some would mind their own business, holding a respectful distance from the natives on whom they knew they were intruding. Others took the opposite approach. Chadwick had arrived early on the evening of the transport, with all the paperwork packed into a box, but this time he was not alone. 'I went to the station accompanied by a Gestapo clerk,' he recalled.[1]

From 7.00 pm, families arrived at the platform, the children wrapped up so tightly to mitigate the cold that their breath was slightly staggered. Chadwick would greet each family with his warm charm, trying to put them at ease in any way he could. 'The mothers did not want to part with their young children,' he observed with some obvious undertones when asked the mood of the parents at that time.[2] He would tick each child off his list, tie a luggage label around their necks and pin an envelope with their name on the front to their lapel for their safekeeping. The documents in the envelope, Chadwick recalled, were 'a large stiff affair, foolscap size, perforated across the middle, with a photograph and all sorts of details on each half'.³ Luggage was kept to a minimum. 'We were allowed one suitcase each, containing only clothes. I remember my main worry being that I might not be allowed to take my love tokens – a collection of small cloth animals,' one child recalled.⁴ All the while, the Gestapo clerk watched on from a courteous distance.

Chadwick also had food prepared for the children to share during the journey. Warriner reminisced that before she had left Czechoslovakia for good, 'Trevor Chadwick and I spent a happy hour packing food for seventy, and carried it to the Wilson station.'⁵ Once a child was registered, had all the right documents and comforts to travel, Chadwick would leave the family to be alone together for what was almost certainly the last time. As one rescued child recollected, after registering, 'we were ushered into an enormous waiting room which was packed with children and parents weeping, crying and shouting'.⁶ The anguish of the parents left a scar with Chadwick for the rest of his life, commenting, 'Good-byes at the train station in Prague were often more difficult and moving when the children had to leave their brothers and sisters behind.'⁷

By 11 pm, 'all the children were there, with labels prepared by my helpers tied round their necks and the train [with thirty-six children aboard] took them off, cheering', was Chadwick's optimistic record of the final part of this section of the rescue.⁸ One girl on the train did not remember it with the same delight: 'From behind the sealed windows I saw my parents, rigid and unsmiling like two statues, for the last time ever.'⁹ There certainly was a lot of cheering from the families left behind, but this was only to put their children at ease as they set off on their adventure. One mother, Chadwick remembered, 'couldn't make up her mind whether to let her little daughter go', so much so that 'three times she pulled her through the window and off the train, and three times she put her daughter back on the train'.¹⁰ Eventually, her daughter did end up leaving on that train, her mother having had the luxury of holding her daughter three more times. For the parents, they could do nothing but return to their home – usually one of the refugee camps – where they would anxiously wait for news of their child's safe arrival in Britain.

The children were not completely alone on the train, as Winton had organised 'half a dozen adult leaders on it', according to a letter Chadwick wrote to one of the children in 1966. Warriner had chosen the adults carefully from her list of Sudeten Germans who were most at risk of Nazi prosecution.[11] This was one of the ways the children's section would help with some of the more clandestine BCRC activities.

With their adult 'supervisors', the children travelled through Germany, where the carriage blinds were firmly closed for the whole journey, then across the border into Holland, before reaching the coast at the Hook of Holland. 'Then came the journey by boat across the channel at night' to Harwich, an 11-year-old passenger told, 'and I remember one little boy in our cabin being violently ill.'[12] For many of the children, this was the first time they had been on a large boat. After arriving on the English coast, the children – by this time completely exhausted after their ordeal – boarded another train, the final leg of their journey to London.

On the morning of 19 April (three days before Chadwick's thirty-second birthday), the train was greeted at Liverpool Street station by Winton and his mother, along with a throng of men, women and children ready to welcome the arrivals into their families. This part of each similar operation was not always one of deep relief and celebration. Winton's impression of this time is that it was fraught. 'Looking back on it now, I really don't quite know how we managed to sort the chaos which ensued when the train pulled in,' he recalled with frustration. 'I remember someone standing on a pile of luggage and shouting out the name of a child and then the name of a guarantor.'[13] There was often a last-minute kerfuffle, with a few children not being properly matched to their foster parents who were present, all of which would eventually be resolved, but caused Winton no end of stress.

So far, the operation was clearly quite an achievement for Winton and Chadwick, who had managed, where many had failed, to bring 156 unaccompanied children out of Czechoslovakia and into safety. Warriner wrote at the time, 'By now there was a perfectly functioning children's organisation [and] I thanked God for Nicky and Chadwick who had got it going against all-round opposition.'[14] However, they both knew that the pace of the rescue needed to pick up, as they had only managed to evacuate a tiny fraction of those they had on their books.

The third train followed quickly, on 29 April, with twenty-nine children. According to both Chadwick and Winton, the train's passengers were all unknowingly travelling with forged documents. Chadwick recalled that he 'could wait no longer [for the real documents] as we had guarantors lined up and the children waiting', so decided to take matters into his own hands.[15] Using his growing underground network in Prague, he 'had some [visas] made, as near as possible like the Home Office ones'.[16] This incredibly risky tactic did pay off and no official was suspicious of the documents, allowing the children to travel safely through Germany before swapping the fakes for the late but real Home Office permits in Holland. Although details of such forgeries are obviously non-existent in the official travel records, Winton confirmed Chadwick's claim in an interview, going further to allude to the fact that this was something he was involved in throughout: 'If [the Home Office] needed that much time to issue visas, I would print them myself.' He did this, he explained, by 'finding a print shop in Prague willing to print false British visas ... the meticulous Germans never spotted the forgeries. They dutifully stamped each one of them, allowing the children to leave the country.'[17] It is difficult to verify this blatant tactic, for apart from the statements from Winton and Chadwick on the topic, none of surviving documents show any sign of forgery. Of course, it could be that they were of such a high quality that real and fake documents can never be told apart, so this will forever remain a mystery. Chadwick – who had a direct and very open line with the top of the Gestapo – had no questions asked of the authenticity of the documents, or about the mission as a whole, for that matter. In one meeting, Bömelburg simply asked him, 'Why do England want so many Jewish children?'[18] In another, British official Robert Stopford was accosted by the Gestapo on the topic: 'The Kriminalrat told me [that] he had discovered that some "dirty Jews" had been forging passports.'[19] Despite this, the matter was not taken any further and no children's transport was negatively impacted. According to Winton's son, his father only engaged in forgeries, 'not really to fool the British government but to just get the permission for the exit visa from the Czech authorities'.[20] In an account several years later, Chadwick referred to the incident of forged documents, stating that after the children had arrived in England, he received a telegram containing 'a threat to send them back', but he paid it no attention as he correctly assumed 'the mob of legally accepted guarantors would stop that'.[21]

Whether travelling on forged documents or not, the second train was able to depart Wilson Station without incident, with six adult 'leaders' aboard. They did encounter a hostile Nazi welcome as the train entered Germany. 'The Nazis boarded the train for a last inspection,' one child recalled, 'pulling down all the suitcases from the racks, opening them and throwing everything on the floor,' before demanding money from each child.[22] Inside the envelopes that Chadwick pinned to each child's lapel would be ten shillings, for emergency use or to fund any onward travel after reaching London. With one last act of cruelty, nine of the ten shillings were taken from each child as a 'fee' for the German soldiers' efforts in searching the train before they could pass through the country. 'Fear was in all of us,' an 11-year-old passenger recalled, with anger in his voice, 'until the moment the whistle blew, the Nazis left, and the train passed over the frontier' to freedom.[23] The following morning, the children arrived safely in London, greeted by the warmth of the Wintons and their new families.

Although the second train arrived without incident, the following day, Bömelburg's driver arrived at Chadwick's office on Voršilská Street with instructions to take him to the Gestapo chief immediately. Chadwick recounted the incident in a letter in the 1960s:

> Bömelburg sent for me. He said people were throwing dust in my eyes. It was now absolutely forbidden for any adult to leave the country without a special *Ausreisebewilligung* and the 'leaders' of my transport had really escaped illegally. I expressed my deepest sorrow and grovelled.[24]

Although, like so many times in his life, Chadwick had expertly charmed his way out of this situation, by illegally putting wanted adults among the children, he was adding a huge risk to their safety.

It appears that from London, Winton was none the wiser of this tactic and would have likely been appalled if he had found out. He made no apology for the fact that the children were his only priority and nothing should jeopardise that.

Within a fortnight of the third train, followed the fourth, and largest, trainload up to that point, which arrived in London on 13 May with sixty-one children aboard. The residents living in Holland on the border with Germany grew accustomed to seeing trainloads of children pulling into the sidings by the Rhine River, shaken and scared after their ordeal of travelling through Germany. By the time the fourth train arrived, the residents were prepared. As the train pulled through the border after yet more unnecessary checks by the Nazi guards, the children were greeted by a group of Dutch women with a large trolley filled with glasses of milk, cups of cocoa, lemonade, fruit, chocolate and sandwiches. 'We were welcomed back to humanity by humanity,' a wise child recalled with tears in her eyes.[25] With their bellies full, the sixty-one children were taken through Holland to the Hook, following the same route as had the previous three trains, getting a boat to Harwich and then a train to their final destination at Liverpool Street station.

Winton managed to increase the pace with the next group – the fifth train – leaving just under a month later, on 2 June, with 123 children, nearly doubling the total number of children evacuated to that point. This train also had a special guest aboard, none other than Trevor Chadwick, who was making a hasty exit from Czechoslovakia. The precise date of his departure is not known but a letter dated from the beginning of June, sent from a new BCRC Prague representative, Beatrice Wellington – who had taken over the reins from Warriner – to Margaret Layton in London, started with the line: 'I am taking advantage of Chadwick's journey to send you this.'[26] Exactly why he left at this point of the operation is not known, although he recalled in a letter that:

> in the evenings there were other fish to fry which did not have anything to do with the children. It became obvious to me as summer developed that certain of my movements were at least suspect, and that [Bömelburg] and his boys might turn sour.[27]

Concerned that this might affect the safety of the children, he 'explained these things to London and they arranged a replacement'.[28]

Chadwick's son, William, had several theories as to why he decided to leave, including an involvement in underground forgeries, hoodwinking the Gestapo or spying for the British. All explanations are plausible, especially the suggestion that he was spying for the British. William points out that 'it would have been amazing if Chadwick had not been approached' by SIS given his close working relationship with senior Nazi officials.[29] He was also closely connected with SIS operative Harold 'Gibby' Gibson, acting as a passport officer, who was known to be actively recruiting agents. Although unsubstantiated, some believed that Chadwick's sudden departure from Prague was down to concern from British officials that he was being turned by the Germans. Winton did not entertain this thought for a second, simply commenting that Chadwick 'deserves all praise'.[30] Regardless of the reason, Chadwick needed to leave suddenly, giving him the opportunity to join one of the train transports he had spent so long organising.

One of the youngsters in Chadwick's train carriage was Tom Schrecker, aged just 7. His uncle, Frank Schrecker, had already fled to London after the Munich Agreement and had spent months desperately trying to help his nephew get to safety. For several days, he would queue at the refugee centre in London, trying to see who could help. Sadly, there were hundreds of people ahead of him in the queue, all trying in vain to do the same. Frank eventually decided to take drastic action, so dressed in a suit and carrying a briefcase as a prop, he walked straight through the reception, confidently heading to the offices. Not speaking any English, he looked for any Czech-sounding names written on the endless doors. Eventually finding one, he knocked and entered a small office to find two women chatting. They initially tried to send him away, but he produced a photo of Tom and pleaded with them for help. As luck would have it, one of these women was Jean Barbour, who immediately offered to take Tom into her home. Just before leaving Prague, Tom's father had arranged for him to be baptised as a Roman Catholic as an extra precaution, also likely at the suggestion of Jean Barbour.

Jean met the train as it arrived on the morning of 3 June, along with the prospective foster parents of the other 122 children and Winton and his entourage. From information given by Tom's father, Jean knew that Tom was a huge animal lover and so the first stop from

Liverpool Street station was London Zoo. From there, they drove to Jean's home in Oxford, where her other two fostered children awaited with excitement the arrival of their new 'brother'. Known as Marnie by her 'children', Jean went on to foster a fourth child, the 3-year-old son of a Polish fighter pilot, who would be killed in the Battle of Britain.

Back in Prague, Tom's mother, Markéta, was one of the millions to be sent to an 'unknown destination' and was never seen or heard of again. She had remained in Prague to care for her sick mother, having divorced Tom's father, with whom Tom was living until his departure for Britain. Tom was one of only a handful of the children who came to England ever to see one of his parents again. His father, Robert, was arrested for making anti-Nazi comments, following a tip-off from one of his disgruntled employees, and was sent to Pankrác Prison. Quite remarkably, his secretary marched into the Gestapo headquarters in the capital and told them that the accusations were false, and demanded his release. What was even more amazing, it worked. He was freed after two months of imprisonment on the condition that he handed over his business to the Nazis, which he of course did. After his release, he fled to China through Italy, where he stayed for the duration of the war before heading to Britain, where he was reunited with his brother and son. Although only imprisoned for two months, the toll on him was so great that it turned his hair completely grey within that short period.

The sixth and largest of the transports comprised 241 children and arrived in Liverpool Street station on 1 July 1939, just under a month after the previous train. The children had left Prague at around midnight on 30 June, waved off by hundreds of family members – by far the largest farewell party of the operation. On the train, 10-year-old Alice Justitzová was smiling eagerly, so excited for her adventure. Not only had she been bought a whole new wardrobe for when she arrived in England, her older sister Mimka had taken her for ice cream with whipped cream on Ruská Street, next to Wilson Station, before she embarked on her journey. As the train began to pull away, Alice noticed her father's lip starting to tremble and tears building up in his eyes. The innocent Alice could do nothing but shout out of the window, 'Daddy, don't spray the platform – you'll embarrass me!'[31] These were the last words she ever spoke to her parents.

Like the previous trains, the children were able to pass through German-occupied Czechoslovakia and into Germany without much bother, until they reached the border. True to form, the Germans decided to search the train. The police walked through the carriages, emptying each child's suitcase onto the floor, kicking the contents around to check for any contraband and taking anything they liked the look of before moving on to the next suitcase. Nine-year-old Amos Ben Ron could not hide his upset at this last act of cruelty, compounded by a feeling of loneliness being without his parents. When he started to wail uncontrollably, his fellow passengers rallied around trying to calm him. An older girl put an arm around his shoulder, squeezed him tight and asked why he was crying.

'I don't know,' Ben replied. 'I just don't feel well.'[32]

Despite the train being in considerable disorder after this affair, it passed safely into Holland. Again, this train was greeted by locals handing out cheese sandwiches and hot cocoa, talking endlessly to the children in Dutch. The children nodded along obligingly, not understanding a word said to them but grateful for the gifts of food and drink and kindness. The group headed on, eventually arriving at London's Liverpool Street station late on 1 July to be greeted by their new foster parents.

What would later become known as the penultimate train left Prague within three weeks, on 19 July. Among the seventy-six children aboard was Vera Lowyova, who managed to squeeze her way through the carriage to a window, where she forced a final glance at her parents. 'My last ever sight of my parents was as they stood behind the barrier, waving their handkerchiefs, while I looked at them out of the train window,' she said.[33]

Once they had pulled away and the train started to pick up speed, 9-year-old Vera found a seat next to a much older child, 16-year-old Mimka Klímová, one of the eldest to travel on the seven trains. Mimka had been booked on the previous journey; however, the only sponsor left for that group of children wanted a girl who was between the ages of 10 and 14. Her 10-year-old sister Alice took her place instead, but now it was Mimka's turn and she was excitedly heading to see her sister. Her parents had made the trip to the station as they had for Alice, and in the same way, Mimka had looked out of the window to see her parents sobbing. Sometimes the forgotten heroes of this story, Winton's son believed, the most courageous of those involved in the transports were not the rescuers, the organisers or the children, but the parents in Prague 'who had the bravery to put their child on a train to send them away' in the hope that their life might be spared.[34] Mimka and Alice's parents certainly demonstrated this, and sadly, they were never to see their children again.

The train took its normal route and the passengers eventually arrived in Britain, tired and apprehensive of what was to happen next. 'I remember sitting on Liverpool Street station in London,' Vera Lowyova recalled, 'hearing announcements in a strange language, seeing children all round me being collected and fearing that I would be left there alone.'[35] She need not have worried, for she was approached by a man and a women who introduced themselves as Leonard and Nancy Faires. The Christian couple had agreed to foster Vera, who was to live with them and their daughter Betty in the English countryside. 'She was very kind,' Vera recalled of Betty, 'kind enough to share her pocket money!'[36]

The final train that was part of the BCRC's children's rescue was due at the end of July. Leaving Wilson Station to the customary cheers, it too passed through occupied Czechoslovakia into hostile

Germany before heading to the Hook of Holland, where the children boarded a ship to take them to Britain. Arriving at Wilson Station along with tens of other children was 9-year-old Milena Fleischmann and her 3-year-old sister Eva, accompanied by their grandmother and mother, as their father was already in England, having made it there on one of the BCRC adult transports. 'My memory of that [day] is very hazy,' Milena recalled in 2016. 'What I do remember is that we only had our backpacks with us, as our cases had been taken away … in the backpacks we had to have enough food for the twenty-four hours it was going to take us to Holland.' In her bag, her mother had added a Czech copy of *The Wind in the Willows* for her to read to her toddler sister Eva, who 'was very quiet', Milena remembered, 'but did not cry'.[37]

The train left Prague with only sixty-six out of the planned sixty-eight children aboard, having to make a stop in Germany to collect 11-year-old Joe Schlesinger and his 9-year-old brother Ernest from Lovosice station. The two boys were forced to wait with their father in the men's toilet at the station, as Jews were not permitted to enter waiting rooms. Joe Schlesinger commented, 'Today, when I look at my own children, I try to imagine even a fraction of the anxiety my father must have felt at the time.'[38] Yet, their father hid all of his angst so well that his children recalled him appearing even cheerful, making jokes as they all squeezed onto a porcelain toilet, waiting for the train to pull in. With a full load, the train then travelled through Germany, taking the longest time out of any of the other trains due to endless checkpoint stops, arriving at the Dutch border only to have their carriages and possessions assiduously searched by the German police. It was to everyone's great relief that they were eventually allowed to leave the country, to be greeted by the Dutch serving them hot cocoa and white bread. This was a food that most of the children had never eaten before. Some described it as tasting wet or like cotton wool, while others threw it out of the window as they headed to the coast.

The train arrived at the Hook of Holland, where they boarded a large steamboat, heading for the safety of the British coast at Harwich. The overnight voyage was slow, but the children were so exhausted from their train journey they were able to sleep, rocked by the waves of the English Channel. For most of them, this was by far the largest boat they had ever seen, but fatigue outweighed any excitement they had felt. They boarded their final train early in the morning, heading for London's Liverpool Street station. The Schlesinger brothers were greeted by Winton's mother, who took them to her house, where they stayed before being collected by their foster parents. A letter exists to this day from their mother thanking Mrs Winton for her hospitality on that first night.

Another two of the sixty-eight children were bothers Hugo and Rudy Maron, aged 11 and 9 at the time. Their arrival was less seamless than that of the Schlesinger boys, as for some reason there was no one waiting to collect them. The brothers waited for hours on the station platform until a taxi driver stopped to ask them if they were okay. In the envelope pinned to their lapel was the name of their guardian, Mr Rabinowitz, who was due to pick them up, but there were no contact details included.

Seeing the boys were hungry, the taxi driver took them to a fish and chip shop for something to eat, the first food they had had since they had regrettably thrown their white bread out of their train window in Holland. The kindly taxi driver then let them stay with his family for a couple of days before finding them an orphanage in Cricklewood, where they stayed for several weeks before finally being collected by some newly assigned foster parents. When asked about these children, Winton could not recall why Mr Rabinowitz never picked them up. Fortunately, the other sixty-six youngsters were collected at the station as planned. Another child on this train, Josef Ginat, was fostered by a Christian minister who was waiting for him at the station. There were many stories of Christians fostering Jewish children, in the hope that they could convert them or, in some cases, only fostering children who had been baptised into the Christian Church before leaving Prague. The minister who looked after Josef did the opposite. He adapted part of his church to resemble a synagogue and bought as much Jewish merchandise as he could lay his hands on, saying, 'I pray in my way, so you should pray in your way.'[39]

On 1 September 1939, a train carrying 251 children, the largest group yet, was cancelled hours before it was due to leave Prague as a result of Germany's invasion of Poland, which would in turn pull Britain into the Second World War. The fate of these children is not known, except for a few who were able escape by alternative means. The others are most likely to have been sent to the Theresienstadt Ghetto and on to Auschwitz, where their plight was devastatingly predictable. The doom of this trainload of children has always hung heavily around Winton's neck. In interviews, he would often find it hard to talk about, as was the case when he spoke to Matej Mináč in 2007:

> We arranged for a transport of 251 children to leave Prague in early September. Can you imagine the scene at the train station that morning? There, the children, their parents and friends gathered to say goodbye. In London, 250 foster parents anxiously awaited their arrival. The children were nearly all aboard, and the train was ready to depart. But it would never leave the station. World War II had broken out, and the rescue mission jolted to a halt. None of the children on the train were ever heard from again. Their life's journey must have ended in some Nazi concentration camp …[40]

When the Nazi terror was brought to an end in 1945, only 14,000 of the estimated 117,000 Jews remained alive in the Czech lands, with the natives being subjected to horrors few could have imagined.

Winston Churchill wrote to his wife Clementine during the war expressing the horror meted out to the country's inhabitants by their occupiers, claiming that 'Czechoslovakians are being as badly treated as one could have expected'.[41] Of the 15,000 children sent to Theresienstadt, just ninety-three were still alive when the camp was liberated. The rest died from starvation, stress, beatings or disease. Knowing that the war was all but lost, SS chief Heinrich Himmler agreed the release of 1,200 Theresienstadt prisoners – including the surviving children – in exchange for 5 million Swiss francs put up by Jewish organisations in an escrowed account in Switzerland.

Chapter 9

The Duration

At 11 am on 3 September 1939, along with most of Britain's population, Winton listened to Neville Chamberlin address the nation from the Cabinet Room in 10 Downing Street. The Prime Minister stated sombrely:

> This morning the British ambassador in Berlin handed the German government a final note stating that unless we heard from them by 11 o'clock that they were prepared at once to withdraw their troops from Poland, a state of war would exist between us. I have to tell you now that no such undertaking has been received, and that consequently this country is at war with Germany.[1]

The effects of those words had a catastrophic impact on the lives of billions, none more so than the children's section of the BCRC. With transports now an impossibility, those who had worked so tirelessly to bring children away from danger were now helpless. They were forced out of their humanitarian line of work, into a life at war.

'I organised an organisation', Winton explained after war was declared, 'to look after the children who we had brought over to see that it was all satisfactory and my mother was in charge of that.'[2] He knew that although there would be no more children coming to Britain, it was essential that those who had been lucky enough to make the journey were taken care of. But the pace of the oncoming war was so intense that after setting the wheels in motion, he said, 'I really did not know anything about it until many years later.'[3]

For so many, the immediate anticipation and anxiety of the declaration led to a huge amount of nervous excitement around the country, despite no actual combat taking place for a while (a time that came to be known as the Phoney War). However, for Winton, his war had been ongoing since the start of the year, when he had touched down in Prague. He wrote to Doreen Warriner at the time, reflecting upon their work together:

> The only trouble with the job in Prague is that after it most other things seem rather flat. You may feel the same. I have got out a rough scheme dealing with the return of refugees to Czechoslovakia after we have won the war. Have you ever thought about it?[4]

Winton was not surprised that Britain had joined the hostilities, as it was something he had continually discussed with his left-wing friends. Along with many, they had seen the inevitably of war as the only solution for Europe. Winton was in a tricky position morally, for he was, deep down, a conscientious objector, but not in the purest form. He explained to his daughter, 'I would be willing to help clear up the mess but not take part in the slaughter.'[5]

Author Ann Kramer defined conscientious objectors as those who ultimately believed it was 'profoundly wrong to kill' because of 'their religious beliefs, political persuasion or for humanitarian reasons'.[6] Winton fell into the last category, as he was not religious, and most political stances towards war at the time were somewhat confused, to say the least.

Winton decided that the best way he could help the war effort without having to fight would be to sign up as a St John Ambulance volunteer. Now working in partnership with the Red Cross, with whom Winton had liaised in Prague, the organisations would go on to provide 249 ambulances, which travelled nearly 6 million miles and carried 681,531 patients during the conflict. Despite still having his job in the City, he decided to help the war effort in a full-time position and take up employment with St John Ambulance. This meant leaving Crews & Company, as unlike his work with the children's rescue, he would not be able to juggle the two. It was the last time he would be involved in the financial services industry, and when war ended, Winton did not go back to the Stock Exchange. He was sickened by the blatant attempts of so many of his former colleagues to profit from the war, and his ethical beliefs meant it was too much of a clash to continue in that industry.

As a full-time St John Ambulance volunteer, Winton's initial remit was setting up a series of Air Raid Precaution (ARP) centres for Hampstead Borough Council. The site selected was a school on Rosslyn Hill, a stone's throw from Winton's Willow Road home. The urgency of the task meant relentless days of organisation until the centre was ready and Winton had to hire a team to work for him. Apart from one incident when an elderly man had swallowed his dentures on the street outside the depot and required first aid, the Phoney War meant the men of the Hampstead ARP unit were twiddling their thumbs.

With nothing to do but wait, and with his proximity to the family home, Winton's activities also included a fair amount of socialising on Willow Road. One guest of particular interest was Wenzel Jaksch, the Sudeten Social Democratic Party leader who had fled Prague in a daring escape dressed as a workman, before skiing his way to freedom into Poland and travelling on to England. Having remained in contact with Winton, he attended a dinner party hosted by Winton's mother, from where Winton, Barbara and Jaksch dashed off a note to Warriner in a rather lubricated style:

> Dear Miss Warriner, we send you the best wishes and greeting from a very nice evening party by Wintons! Yours W. Jaksch.

The evening party is degenerating, as Mr Jaksch is staying the night on account of 'noises off', love Barbara Winton.

Hope you will join one of our jovial bomb parties one day! Am just up for a few days' holiday, but shall return for a rest! Good luck, Nicky.[7]

After six months in post, Winton felt he had achieved all he could in his job at Rosslyn Hill and needed a change, so he signed up as an ambulance driver for the Red Cross, a partner of St John Ambulance. The job of a driver was somewhat ambiguous, as it was unclear where Winton would serve, whether it be around Britain or overseas. With the hasty retreat of the British Expeditionary Force through Europe to Dunkirk, Winton's fluent French made his candidature appealing. After expressing his interest, 'I had been called by them within 10 days,' he recalled. He was lucky to have been contacted, as 'through some muddle at HQ' many of those who had registered before him were not called.[8]

Upon being called, Winton's position was confirmed and he was subsequently put through a hasty Red Cross training programme, which he passed on 11 March 1940. His qualification stated that he had been 'found to be proficient in accordance with the regulations of the Society [and] is entitled to wear the Red Cross Badge'.[9] Winton's daughter explained that he had little time to celebrate, as the drivers were busy ensuring 'their ambulances [were] all polished with shiny bright chrome' as they were due to be presented to a VIP.[10] On 15 March 1940, along with other ambulance drivers, Winton drove into London to be inspected by the King in the quadrangle at Buckingham Palace. 'Royal interest in Ambulance Unit' read the front-page headline of the *Nottingham Journal* the following day. The newspaper explained how 'the King and Queen inspected the first ambulance unit [which] will shortly leave for France'.[11]

Immediately after their dalliance with royalty, Winton was sent to Boulogne in France to help with the withdrawal of British soldiers making their way to Dunkirk. He was somewhat put out that when he drove off the boat onto the shore of France, he was told to source dark paint and cover the beautiful shine of their vehicles they had so lovingly buffed for the King and Queen. Now they were in combat, it was not the time to be driving around in a beacon that would likely attract attention from the Luftwaffe pilots swarming overhead. Winton explained that because the vehicles they were driving had 'large chromium-plated bumpers, two windows each side and two at the back, all with one-inch chromium plate beading', it meant that although 'they looked beautiful, [they] could be seen for miles'.[12] Somewhat reluctantly, Winton got on with the new paint job, working with his assigned co-driver, called Mummery.

As drivers, Winton and Mummery's job was only to transport the injured, as they received very little basic medical training. This meant that they were unable to help those whom they were driving in any medical way, which caused a lot of confusion, irritation and upset. This was a continual source of frustration for the unit, which Winton tried to address. He wrote in a report about his time with the organisation: 'I did my best to arrange First Aid classes, but after an interview with the officer responsible … he told [me] he did not believe in them [so] I gave up the unequal struggle.'[13] The Red Cross had handed out 298,343 certificates to those who had successfully completed their first aid training courses by the time of the Dunkirk evacuation, yet decided that their drivers were not worthy or capable of this knowledge.

Winton's first experience of action came while driving in convoy between Boulogne and Calais, where Luftwaffe planes attacked the vehicles, spraying bullets at them. Winton and Mummery were able to slam the breaks on and dive into the ditch on the side of the road, only to return to their ambulance to find the cab full of bullet holes.

Upon seeing this, they were less upset about having been forced to paint it.

For several hectic days, Winton drove through gunfire and bombing, delivering wounded men back to field hospitals. During a rare period of rest, he was able to try to fix up his ambulance following its shower of 30 mm calibre bullets courtesy of a German airman.

After only a matter of weeks of being in France, along with 25,000 other men in St Nazaire, Winton found himself waiting patiently to be evacuated before being whisked home to Britain on a very long and uncomfortable journey. Before reaching the boat, his convoy had been halted west of Calais, where the two officers in charge of his unit had gone ahead, telling Winton and the others that they would soon be back to collect them. When no one returned, one of the drivers took it upon himself to guide the group onwards, which he successfully did, allowing them to escape on one of the waiting boats. Winton's daughter commented that at this point, 'Nicky and the others in their team felt they were nearly home but due to the weather conditions it took four days to arrive in Plymouth.'[14]

Only when Winton arrived back to the shores of Britain did he learn that the two officers from his convoy who had gone on ahead had left France as soon as they got to the coast, leaving the rest of the party to fend for themselves. Understandably, this upset Winton and his fellow volunteers, so much so that 90 per cent of the unit resigned when they arrived back in Britain. 'Out of the original 50 [men] inspected by the King and Queen at the Palace, there are now only 5 left,' exclaimed Winton in a report he wrote about his time in France.[15]

Winton was more forgiving than those who left, and remained working for the Red Cross. With little ambulance driving required overseas, Winton was sent to Sussex, where he drove his ambulance through the worst days of the Blitz and the Battle of Britain.

Air battles over Sussex were rife when Winton arrived, with the brave men of the Royal Air Force desperately trying to stave off the Luftwaffe aggression. Resident Mrs Ramsey remembered events that took place from the first day that fighting started where Winton was stationed:

> I saw the first air battle overhead ... the Battle of Britain was on. ... By August we had terrific raids [and] 140 German planes were shot down that day. On 24 August, a further 800 planes came over and there were some fierce battles. Air battles went on all day and at night as well, bombs dropping till 3.30 am when we got our first sleep'[16]

Winton was right in the middle of the action, ferrying wounded people from the rubble of their homes to hospital, trying to navigate the pitch-dark roads with dimmed headlights due to the blackout. Given the battle was taking place in the sky, Winton would often be called upon to pick up a wounded Luftwaffe pilot, with whom he would be able to communicate in German, making for some interesting conversations.

It was not just the fighting in the air that kept Winton and his Red Cross colleagues busy, as being located in the county meant the area was often used as a dumping ground by enemy bombers returning from their attacks on London, leaving some of the residents suffering the collateral damage. News of the destruction became an all too frequent storyline, with the *Mid-Sussex Times* reporting in early 1941: 'The weekend blitz on London resulted, as on previous raids, in a number of bombs being unloaded from enemy planes in Mid-Sussex.'[17]

Often, Winton and his colleagues were called to a bombsite as a raid was still in progress, to collect the victims who had been pulled out from the rubble of what used to be their homes and take them to hospital. Like in France, none of the drivers were given any medical training, which became an acute problem when they arrived at an area full of injured people only to have to turn away anyone seeking immediate help. 'As we naturally had Red Crosses all over ourselves,' Winton explained, 'the inability of the vast majority of our number to render any kind of First Aid was often commented upon.'[18]

After eighteen months in the Red Cross, Winton had had enough; as when he was with the ARP, he wanted to do something new. 'His level of activity in the Red Cross was no longer what he felt he should be doing,' his daughter explained. 'There was not enough real action and he was not doing enough good, and on top of that he was bored,' as well as frustrated by his inability to provide any medical care.[19]

The taste of action was enough for him to change his stance as a conscientious objector of sorts. His time in Sussex had given him the chance to meet many brave members of the RAF, some of whom he had picked up in his ambulance after they had been shot down, and this piqued his interest. On top of this, there was a groundswell of admiration for the RAF, spurred on by the Prime Minister's continued praise, with speeches stating such perspectives as 'the gratitude of every home in our island … goes out to the British airmen'.[20] Buoyed with all the hype, in late 1941 Winton attended one of the volunteer application days to join the RAF, along with hundreds of other men eager to take part in the action. The recruitment brochure declared: 'The qualifications you require as an applicant for air crew services [are that] you must be physically fit, intelligent, and have a desire to fight in the air.'[21]

Although Winton believed he possessed the necessary attributes to sign up – now even a desire to fight – he was turned down because of his poor eyesight. Something that became a trademark of his appearance, Winton's circular glasses instantly raised concern as he entered the recruitment office.

Undiscouraged, he decided to remain at the event and apply for non-flying duties within the RAF. He was an ideal candidate for a position as a flight trainer for all the new recruits that were being signed on in droves. After the fall of France in 1940, aircraft production had become one of the most pressing issues for the country. On 15 May that year, Air Chief Marshal Sir Hugh Dowding commented about the losses the British were experiencing at the hands of the Luftwaffe, saying, 'If the present rate of wastage continues for another fortnight, we shall not have a single [aircraft] left.'[22] This led the newly appointed Minister of Aircraft Production, Lord Beaverbrook, to significantly and effectively increase the rate of aeroplane construction, increasing the fleet by 28 per cent from 565 available craft on 22 June to 721 by 2 November. Despite this success, 'hundreds of new aircraft every week are valueless by themselves', stated the RAF recruitment material, and 'there must be crews to man them'.[23]

With the recruitment drive in full force, Winton agreed to join as part of a pilot training programme, helping to rapidly upskill the new airmen. Sent to Hatfield in Hertfordshire, Winton was an instructor for one of the first flight simulators, called the Link Trainer, which would teach pilots night flying without having to actually enter an aircraft.

The *Courier and Advertiser* described the device as 'one of the most important lessons which a new pilot entering the RAF has to undergo'.[24] Winton's language skills were called upon once again, as he was assigned the task of training French pilots who had escaped from their occupied country and were keen to fight back. With increased bombing raids at night, training for flying in darkness was essential, while being difficult and very time-consuming to teach in actual aircraft. Winton's contribution to the RAF continued as he was re-posted to the South Cerney aerodrome in Gloucestershire for more Link training.

He met a former school friend, the wonderfully named Geoffrey de Havilland Jnr., who was a qualified Spitfire pilot. Geoffrey agreed to take Winton on a flight, allowing him to escape the simulator and experience the true sensation. Squeezed into the cockpit between his friend's legs, Winton had to grip on for dear life as Geoffrey manoeuvred loop-the-loops and barrel rolls. The flight left Winton shaken and all too willing to remain on terra firma.

Following the Imperial Japanese Navy Air Service's attack on Pearl Harbor on 7 December 1941 and the subsequent entry of the Americans into the war, victory over the Axis Powers became more of a reality. Meanwhile, Winton's time in South Cerney continued until 1944, when he was assigned to a special group of RAF representatives to take the Link as an exhibition around Europe.

It is somewhat strange that such an activity was seen as being of enough importance to send a group of RAF specialists around the Continent while war was still being furiously fought. Winton's daughter surmised, 'It was obviously considered a valuable propaganda device, as it progressed across Europe in the wake of the Allied advance through Belgium, France and Germany.'[25] Besides this, the device had also created such a buzz, with the *Illustrated London News* hailing the Link Trainer as 'one of the most ingenious devices devoted to the modern training of pilots, one which enables them to be taught to fly blind without leaving the ground or even going out of doors'. There was a lot of demand from other countries to adopt the machine.[26]

Along with his fellow RAF colleagues, Winton visited six cities over the space of fifteen months, where he witnessed the destruction of war first hand. He described how, in many places, 'I did not see one house undamaged and few enough with their walls standing. ... It is far worse than I had ever imagined and to be in the midst of so much ruin was terrifying.'[27]

The devastation was contrasted with the excitement of locals at finally being free of Nazi rule, meaning that Winton – before having to return to his quarters in time for the midnight curfew – was indulged with concerts, theatre visits and restaurants (if the establishment had any food to offer). While in Brussels at the end of November 1944, Winton wrote excitedly to his mother about a 19-year-old woman he had met on one of his many social evenings. 'Having in the first weeks met crowds of girls, I have during the last week been going around with one in particular,' he exclaimed. They would go to events together; one theatre visit he critiqued as 'not a good play or particularly well acted' but did concede the night was not a total disaster as 'a play in a foreign language is always interesting'.[28] Unfortunately, Winton's travel schedule meant that he was back on the road and on to another city without his female acquaintance.

It was on this tour that he returned to Prague for the first time since his three weeks in the city at the start of 1939. Despite having written many letters home to his mother while travelling, his daughter said there was surprisingly no mention in any of them about Prague. There was a telegram sent to the British Air Ministry, which explains that 'Winton has valuable pre-war contacts [in Prague] which are proving of immense help'.[29] It was a strange experience for everyone on this tour, as they got to see communities getting to grips with supposed freedom for the first time in about four years. Demonstrations and strikes started to flare up in the cities that Winton visited, which were aimed mainly at a lack of basics such as available jobs, healthcare or food. Winton explained to his mother in a letter: 'They do not realise it but they are suffering from four years of German propaganda. ... The only thing they have practised for years and can do well is to break laws.'[30]

During this visit in Prague, one of Winton's colleagues was taken seriously ill with diphtheria – a major bacterial infection – from which he died. With the grim task of taking the body back to Britain, the irony was not lost on Winton that nearly five years after he was saving the lives of children by having them escorted out of Prague to

Britain, he found himself on a plane sitting next to a coffin. On the journey, he was able to sneak a set of engraved Czech wine glasses back, which is now a family heirloom. Where he hid them on that plane ride remains a mystery.

Chapter 10

Peacetime

The end of the war meant demobilisation for Winton and a return to civilian life. He was committed to the pledge he had made in 1939 that he would not return to the City and the world of finance. Despite being a very competent stockbroker, the outlook and ethics of these types of organisations were not in line with Winton's own worldviews. Instead, he applied for a position with the International Committee for Refugees in London. The *Manchester Evening News* reported that the committee was 'concerned with the future of the stateless and those who cannot bring themselves to return to the land from which they have been driven'.[1]

Only a matter of five years previously, Winton had no humanitarian or refugee aid experience, but his time in Prague and subsequently the BCRC had triggered a desire for him to do more. To be accepted into the International Committee for Refugees, Winton relied on a reference provided by Doreen Warriner, which she wrote with much generosity:

To whom it may concern.
Mr N.G. Winton acted as my assistant in Prague in the winter of 1938/39, under the British Committee for Refugees from Czechoslovakia. ... He was solely responsible for the successful development of a large organisation controlling the migration of children from Czechoslovakia in large numbers, and he himself raised the considerable financial resources from private and government funds. In his work he showed great sense of

responsibility, enterprise and organising ability and in situations of extreme difficulty in Prague he showed great qualities of tact, decision and reliability.[2]

Her reference had its desired effect and Winton was accepted, thanks in no small part again to his language abilities. His new job sent him as part of a three-person team to the Swiss city of Geneva, where he would be headquartered. Notorious for its expensive living, Winton found himself in a fortunate position as he was paid an American rate salary with no income tax deductions, meaning he was suddenly very well off, even by Switzerland's standards. The reasoning behind this was that while in Geneva, he was seconded into the United Nations.

Winton's first assignment was to go to Frankfurt to help the logistics of resettling refugees in a displacement camp. The city was an absolute disaster zone, as Winton remembered from his visit when working for the RAF, with very few buildings still resembling their original structure. With the damaged infrastructure and endless American checkpoints throughout the city, travel was often very drawn out and somewhat frustrating for Winton.

Most of the locals Winton met, he recalled, were living out of their basements beneath the ruins of their houses. Similar to his time in Prague in early 1939, Winton had a strong feeling of guilt that whilst everyone around him was living in ruins, he was staying in one of the only buildings that was fully intact – a hotel that appeared to be running as if the war had never happened.

Within Frankfurt, he took on the task of supervising the liquidation of Nazi assets that had been stolen during the Holocaust. This involved the collection of anything from jewellery and clothing to gold fillings from teeth. Winton would pick up loot, usually reported through anonymous tips, have it broken down into basic materials, checked by experts to confirm authenticity and then negotiate the best price for it and accumulate the money. The proceeds, worth over $25 million, were then sent back to Europe for distribution to help communities persecuted by the Nazis to be given the chance of resettlement and rehabilitation, in accordance with the Five Power Agreement. Winton used his blossoming hobby as a photographer to record the process, from when boxes were opened through to when the contents were repurposed. He would later state that of all his life experiences, this would 'stay in my memory forever'.[3] Travelling forty-three times between Germany, France, Switzerland and America in eight months, Winton was the Deputy of Reparations, working under the Head of Reparations, a man called Abba Schwartz. The Harvard Law School-educated owner of his own legal practice had chosen Winton for such a senior position for his bilingual communication ability and his background in financial services. Schwartz was an inspirational man to Winton, becoming Assistant Secretary of State for Security and Consular Affairs in 1962 under President John F. Kennedy, and had been a close ally and advisor to Eleanor Roosevelt.

As Director of Reparations, Schwartz needed someone to whom he could deputise a lot of his operational work, and he chose Winton for that task. Included in the material he had to deal with were non-personal items, such as blocks of gold and money, but the reality really set in when he would be presented with a military box, which upon opening, contained gold teeth and fillings that had been prised from the jaws of executed Jews in concentration camps. This box was followed by another filled with wedding rings, another with dentures, another with women's jewellery, another with pairs of glasses, and possibly the most horrific of all, some filled with children's toys that the Nazis must have thought to be of particular value. For Winton, it was hard not to image these toys belonging to many of the 5,000 children he had originally hoped to save, 4,000 of whom were thought to have perished in gas chambers. It was this experience that led Winton to say about his humanitarian efforts: 'I have often been unwilling to speak about the rescue mission because [I] felt guilty that I couldn't do more for the children who I couldn't get out.'[4]

A lot of the valuable material had been 'dispersed for protection in the spring of 1945', *The Scotsman* reported in late 1946. The newspaper gives an insight into the lengths that the retreating Nazis had gone to in order to squander their loot from the advancing Allies: 'More than six months were spent tracing the documents before a list of targets could be drawn up for the raids. Valuables had been moved so frequently that some records when found were useless.'[5] Coordinated raids recovered a huge number of valuable items for Winton, but it is thought to this day, there are still small fortunes yet to be found.

In total, Winton accompanied 844 crates of items for sale to America, the contents of which included silver, rugs, china, watches and even collectable postage stamps. Also on board were hundreds of crates containing worthless items, such as fake diamonds. In order to dispose of these to ensure they were not profited from in any way, Winton had the ship's crew smash the crates open with sledgehammers and then the worthless loot would be scattered overboard, the closest their deceased owners would get to a dignified burial. Winton told his daughter that for him, while working on this 'day after day and week after week, one had to separate oneself from the emotional side of how and why and when all this happened and concentrate in dealing entirely with the practical job in hand'.[6] It was this stiff-upper-lip mentality that had guided him eight years earlier when arranging the evacuations of children from Prague. It is hard to find a criticism of Winton, but comments have been made about his objective view of humanitarian aid, for example, providing photo cards of children allowing prospective foster parents to choose the child to whom they would offer a home, in a similar way to how one picks out a household pet. The reality was that his ability to keep his emotions in check and focus on the task in front of him allowed Winton success throughout his life. Today it is an unfortunate British stereotype to have your feelings suppressed and keep a stiff upper lip, but after the war, this was expected. Certainly, part of the reason Winton was not forthcoming about his achievements with the BCRC was because of this attitude.

Disposing of the Nazi loot kept Winton busy until 1948, when he conducted his last task as Deputy of Reparations, escorting a huge sum of Nazi cash in many different currencies to Julius Baer Merchant Bank in Zurich. While working for the International Committee for Refugees, Winton returned to Prague for a reunion with members of the BCRC. Warriner wrote of the schedule in her diary: 'Martin Blake to dinner tomorrow. Nicky was here too.'[7] It was strange for Winton to be back with those with whom he had worked before the war, not least because most of them had spent nearly a year in the city, whereas Winton had only been there for a matter of weeks.

What was evident to everyone returning to Prague was the level of suffering its people had been through since they were last there. The physical destruction was all around, with the famous buildings such as the Emmaus Monastery, Faust House and Vinohrady Synagogue in ruins. But the infrastructure was insignificant to the former members of the BCRC, as they struggled to track down any of their Czech contacts, most of whom had either been killed or deported, or had disappeared. The country was not only suffering from the aftermath of Nazi rule, but also the Communist Party of Czechoslovakia (KSČ) had held a successful Soviet-backed coup in February 1948 to gain control of the country. Winton witnessed the loss of Eastern Europe's democracy – a symbol of the start of the Cold War.

After his brief, depressing respite in Prague, during the second quarter of 1948 Winton found himself in need of another job. He successfully applied for a role in Paris, joining the International Bank for Reconstruction and Development (IBRD). What would eventually morph into the World Bank, the IBRD set out a bold ambition from its inception: 'Our dream is a world free of poverty,' was their proudly stated motto.[8] The bank was established as a lending cooperative for middle-income developing countries, mainly those that had been devastated by conflict. The opportunity for Winton was almost too good to be true, as he had sworn he would never re-enter the banking world, but here was a chance to put the skills he had learnt while operating as a stockbroker to use, but in a way that would help those in serious need around Europe. As with many of his other jobs, his language skills were a major factor in his selection.

He joined the IBRD on 1 April 1948, at a time when the bank was under huge strain to provide aid before it was too late. 'In this critical interval necessary for recovery,' warned British Chancellor of the Exchequer Hugh Dalton, 'there are grave dangers in many countries of economic collapse and social dissolution.' The IBRD 'faced a grave challenge as the tides of fate are fast running out', he concluded.[9] It was against this pressing backdrop that Winton started his position as a supervisor in the Treasurer's department. This job was less emotionally draining for Winton, but he still had huge responsibility on his slender, 38-year-old shoulders, with the remit of supervising the distribution of $250 million loaned by the US to the French bank Crédit National. A small fraction of the $20 billion dollars loaned to Europe in what became known as the Marshall Plan was provided on the advice of the newly formed Central Intelligence Agency (CIA) under the premise that 'the greatest danger to the security of the United States is the possibility of economic collapse in western Europe and the consequent accession to power of communist elements'.[10]

'I suppose that this posting of all the things which I have done in life had the greatest consequence, insofar as it was there that I met my wife,' Winton told his daughter.[11] Grete Gjelstrup was a curiously attractive 28-year-old woman from Denmark, who was secretary to the director of the IBRD, the man for whom Winton worked. Winton was immediately taken with Grete for many reasons, not least because the work he was embarking on was mundane in comparison to that of the previous ten years of his life, leading him to easy distraction and a desire for excitement. He was, after all, in the world's most romantic city. She, on the other hand, did not take to him very well at the start. Believing that she was his secretary as well – despite this never actually having been said – Winton turned up at her desk soon after he started at the IBRD and asked her to type a letter. Somewhat taken aback, Grete was professional and obliged. When Winton cleared his throat and started by dictating: 'Dear Mother. Thank you for the coffee pot you sent …' Grete couldn't believe her ears. The impertinence, she thought. She was not only being treated as his secretary, but he was using her to run his personal errands. It was never said whether Grete actually finished the letter, but it was a story that she enjoyed telling.

Luckily for Winton, this episode did not hinder their friendship, which blossomed quickly, to the point where they would often see each other socially outside of the office. This included visiting churches, attending operas and viewing those galleries that were still standing all around Paris. Winton was the louder and more outgoing of the pair, whereas Grete liked to be more reserved, acting as a sponge to her surroundings. 'She possessed an enormous curiosity about the world,' their daughter explained.[12] It was perhaps this that led Grete to agree to watch Winton in various fencing competitions he had signed up for in Paris, which, for the onlooker, were long, tedious and far from thrilling.

They had been together for just five months when, while enjoying dinner with a friend near the Gare du Nord, Winton was hit by the impulse to marry Grete. Leaving the table, and his friend, he rushed out into the street, flagged down a passing taxi and asked to be taken to Grete's flat. The pounding on the door in the dead of night was in no way romantic, and terrified poor Grete, who had been fast asleep. Her landlady was summoned to act as security as she cautiously approached the door and asked who was there. When it transpired that it was Winton, her thoughts turned from fear to alarm, as the only explanation for him being there in such a fluster at that time of night was that some type of disaster had struck. When he was allowed in, Winton began his hastily prepared proposal to Grete, who stood shocked in her nightdress, while the beady eyes of her landlady watched on. The slightly unorthodox proposal nevertheless worked, and Grete agreed to give him her hand in marriage.

Like the impulsiveness of his proposal, the newly engaged couple set a date for their wedding for just seven weeks ahead. This was a challenge for their guests as they also decided that it would take place in Denmark. The wedding, on 31 October 1948, was, as per the local custom, a lavish three-day affair, with banquets for every lunch and dinner hosted by various members of Grete's family. 'My greatest happiness I suppose was when I got married,' Winton reminisced to a Norwegian reporter years later.[13] As Winton's oldest friend, Stanley Murdoch acted as best man for the couple.

With the festivities completed, the Wintons returned to Paris, where they found an apartment on the Rue de Passy, one of the oldest streets in the beautiful former village of Passy, and the past home to famous philosopher Pierre-Joseph Proudhon – a fact Winton enjoyed relating to visitors. Their tiny flat had limited facilities, but this did not stop them from hosting dinner parties, where they cooked food on a homemade spit over their open fire. One guest was Jean Weidner, who had founded the Dutch-Paris underground organisation, which was responsible for the escape of 800 Dutch Jews and 112 Allied pilots to Switzerland. Like Winton, Weidner's modesty meant they did not discuss their wartime experiences, instead focusing on more traditional dinner topics, such as politics. Despite the very primitive cooking arrangements, Grete was taking lessons at a local Cordon Bleu cookery school, meaning the meals in the Winton household soon became heavily sought-after. For the rest of her life, Grete was renowned for her culinary prowess, being particularly popular years later with their children's friends.

In October 1949, Winton's contract with the IBRD ended. He decided that this was the perfect time for the not so newlyweds to have their honeymoon. They chose the United States because, not only were they curious to explore the land of the free, but Winton had been paid in US dollars, which had an incredibly bad exchange rate. He therefore had a lot of cash to spend and only one place in which to do so.

Feeling flush, Winton booked the couple into one of 577 RMS *Queen Mary* tourist class cabins for their transatlantic crossing. Joining them aboard was brooding actor Errol Flynn, whose recently signed fifteen-year contract with Warner Brothers for $225,000 per film meant he had the best suite on the ship – a far cry from the Wintons' third-class accommodation.

Starting in New York, the couple rented a car and drove nearly 1,500 miles through Tennessee, Alabama, New Orleans and Florida, primarily on the north–south Route 65. 'The roads are all good, and most excellent,' Winton wrote to his mother. 'Everyone exceeds the speed limit and the story of traffic policemen chasing all speeders is a myth.'[14] Winton had become apt at driving at considerable speed while behind the wheel of his ambulance, so he was in his element on these roads. The couple spent a happy four weeks travelling through America, lapping up the culture.

A month after arriving in the United States, the Wintons returned to reality with a bump as they arrived back in Britain and the damp spring weather. The couple's carefree travelling honeymoon had come at a literal cost, having burnt through all of Winton's IBRD earnings. With next to nothing to his name, most pressing for Winton was that he needed to find a new job. Luckily, his mother Barbara was on hand with a suggestion.

'I played bridge with a gentleman yesterday', she told him, 'who has started a factory in Maidenhead making ice cream and he is looking for someone with financial knowledge.'[15]

Barbara arranged for the man – named Guy Lawrence – to have a meeting with her son, which went so well that he offered him the role of finance director on the spot for his new company, Glacier Foods. This meant the Wintons needed to find a home in Maidenhead, and the area suited the couple perfectly. They discovered a modest detached house called Dodbrook, just outside the town centre in a cul-de-sac called Altwood Bailey, and with a 2 per cent mortgage, the property was theirs in exchange for £1,460.

Based in Dodbrook, the couple went on to have three children: Nick, born on 27 July 1952, Barbara, on 23 October 1953, and Robin, who was born on 14 August 1956 with Down's syndrome. In the 1950s, Down's syndrome was seen as more debilitating to the parents than the child, so the immediate advice to Winton and Grete was that Robin should live in care rather than return home to be with his family. The Wintons did not accept this and instead decided they would care for Robin themselves, a decision they never once regretted. Along with two dogs called Whiskey and Chip and a cat named Ginger, the family lived happily, albeit with the incredible strain of bringing up a disabled child.

Adding to the stress, Winton's relationship with his mother had started to deteriorate when he married Grete, of whom Barbara did not approve. Barbara was also very perturbed by Robin, finding it hard for her to feel she could visit her grandchildren. Sadly, it was widely believed that a child born with disabilities was in some way linked to the moral compass of the parents. Winton's mother simply could not get her head around what had happened to Robin and why he was how he was. Nevertheless, Winton worked hard on the relationship and managed to stay close with her. He went so far as to offer her an allowance each year to cover her somewhat lavish living expenses in her Baker Street apartment.

In 1958, the Wintons moved into a new house, which was literally that. They had purchased a piece of land 3 miles outside Maidenhead and built a Scandi-style home for £9,000. The family were in paradise, surrounded by sprawling, unspoiled countryside meaning the children had a giant playground in which to spend their days. 'If it sounds wonderful, it was,' exclaimed their daughter.[16]

Their happiness would not last, for the day before his sixth birthday, Robin died suddenly. In the hope of protecting their other children, Winton and Grete had the funeral without Nick and Barbara – who were both away from home on holiday – knowing their brother had died. As a distraction to the heartache of losing a child, Winton kept himself busy at work, helping to negotiate the sale of Glacier Foods to the largest ice cream producer in Britain, Lyons. On the side of this, he unsuccessfully set up a venture to provide hire purchase agreements, but this business quickly collapsed.

In 1965, Winton sent his eldest child, Nick, aged 13, to a boarding school named Abingdon, as this was something he had always wanted for his son. Nick hated his time away from home and would often be in tears when being driven back after the school holidays. Winton did not bend to his son's protestations that he despised being away from home, leaving Nick to sit it out. Winton had some sympathy, having struggled being away from his parents at Stowe School, but he had found the experience so valuable that he wanted his son to have the same. Barbara, on the other hand, went to the local girl's grammar school, which she thoroughly enjoyed, so much so that when Winton suggested she might spend her sixth form at Marlborough College, she begged him to allow her to remain where she was.

The early 1970s signalled a major change for the Wintons, as both their children left home for good, leaving Nicky and Grete alone. Winton had always loved having the house full and entertaining Nick and Barbara's friends for sleepovers and parties. Their fleeing the nest coincided with Winton's decision that this was the right time for him to retire from full-time work at the somewhat early age of 62 and focus more on his charity endeavours. He had recently left Lyons to start work for a friend who owned a sheet metal company based on the Slough Trading Estate. However, things did not work out there and Winton quickly saw the writing on the wall that the business was on a downward trajectory. He therefore resigned and decided to retire from commercial life.

Winton's first year of retirement was spent focused on politics, as he decided to join and later became chairman of the local Labour Party in Maidenhead. The heavily Tory area did not allow Winton his ambition of election to public office; the closest he got was when he achieved a 41.3 per cent share of the vote in the Maidenhead Borough Council Election on 13 May 1954.

Deciding politics was not after all for him, he hung up his red Labour rosette and set his sights on charity. He and Grete had been helped by the charity Mencap with caring for Robin's disabilities, for which Winton had helped establish the Maidenhead branch. He became the local chairman and served on the national committee. Winton also volunteered for the Samaritans and became volunteer chairman of the Abbeyfield Society, a charity providing accommodation for the elderly. He quickly expanded the enterprise, organising the erection of Hardwick House in Abbeyfield, Winton House in Windsor in 1980, and Nicholas House in 2011. He retained an active role in the society for the rest of his life, serving as their president until his death. 'He is remembered fondly for his attitude of just getting things done,' the charity commented, 'as well as his ability to persuade others into carrying out work on his behalf' – a trait he unashamedly used to carry out his 1939 rescue operation.[17]

In 1983, Winton's friend Stanley Pratt nominated him for an MBE for his charity work. The family attended the ceremony at Buckingham Palace, watching him finally receive a bit of recognition for his life's most important work. This award would, however, be eclipsed by what was to follow. Five years later, Winton was invited to attend a recording of *That's Life* – an experience that would change his life for ever. The first major article to appear about his work in saving children was in the *Sunday Mirror* on 28 February 1988, with a three-page spread titled 'The Lost Children. Little refugees left waiting for their brave Pied Piper'.[18] From that point, Winton's life took a different trajectory, as he was rightly given multiple honours for what he had achieved, including the freedom of Prague, the Order of Tomáš Masaryk and a knighthood. Winton used his meteoric rise to fame to promote causes close to his heart and spread his philosophy around the world. 'Be prepared always', he told a group of Slovak children in 1999, 'to help other people if there is an opportunity to do so.'[19]

The recognition he received came at a price, taking Winton from a life of relative anonymity to huge fame. At its peak, tragedy struck him with the death of Grete on 28 August 1999. Fifty-one years of having Grete at his side suddenly came to an abrupt end. 'I can't imagine how he was when he was alone,' his daughter reflected, 'but he soldiered on,' as he always had.[20]

Winton celebrated his 100th birthday by flying a microlight over White Waltham Airfield. 'It was quite turbulent, but he didn't mind,' pilot Judy Leden reported afterwards.[21] Leden was not unaware of how precious was her cargo on that flight, for seventy years earlier, her father, Tom Leden, had escaped the Nazis in Prague on one of Winton's trains.

At the remarkable age of 106, on 1 July 2015, having been admitted to Wexham Park Hospital in Slough due to his deteriorating health, Winton died peacefully. He was buried alongside Grete and Robin, with a typically understated gravestone simply stating names and dates. Nevertheless, by the time of his death, the mention of Winton's name was all that was needed to understand the impact he had had on the world.

Epilogue

Winton was never shy about the fact that, as he said in one speech before his death in 2015, 'most of the credit should go to others'.[1] Of the 'others', the two outstanding names were those of Doreen Warriner and Trevor Chadwick. In honour of Winton's view that the credit should go to them, a brief summary of their lives after the Prague operation is provided.

Chadwick had been unsure what to do when the war started, actually turning to Warriner for advice. In what appears to be the only letter he wrote to her after leaving the BCRC, he stated:

> I admit I should rather like a commission, thus getting a smart uniform and being saluted, heil Chadwick and getting tight on gin very cheap and wasting Admiralty money with a happy smile. If you know of something more useful to do in this quaint war, I would do it. Can you give me any hints?[2]

It does not appear that Warriner gave him any hints, so he decided on a career in the Royal Navy Reserve and was posted on the requisitioned steam ship HMS *Mollusc*, which was sunk shortly after. Determining life at sea was not for him, he joined the RAF instead. As a flying officer, his work was mostly desk-based, which caused him little satisfaction. Guy Phelps, one of the children he rescued when he first arrived in Prague, commented that Chadwick 'had a chequered subsequent life and career, at one point joining the RAF, where he was both court-martialled and [later] promoted'. His disciplinary offence was absence without leave, which was time spent drinking – a pastime that sadly engulfed a lot of his life.

His promotion to flight lieutenant was unfortunately short-lived as, on 25 February 1942, he crashed his military jeep while drunk when posted in Africa and was invalided back to Britain. He was diagnosed with anxiety and depression, resulting in his dismissal for being 'found below required standard' for the RAF. Life for Chadwick was not particularly happy after this, with his separation from his wife, remarriage and then separation from his second wife. For ten years, he worked in various careers, including being a landlord, a driver and working in gambling. After his second divorce, Chadwick became critically ill with tuberculosis, which nearly cost him his life.

It was his move to Norway that put his life back on track. In Oslo, he resumed his teaching career before founding the Oslo University Press with friends, which he enjoyed until he retired aged 68 and moved back to Britain. Back in Southampton, Chadwick met Sigi, his third wife, whom he was with for the rest of his life. Sadly, Chadwick was again struck down by illness, this time a stroke, which led to medical issues in hospital and his eventual death in 1979, aged 72.

After his death, in a letter dated 28 March 1999, Winton wrote:

> I am delighted to hear that, at long last, Trevor Chadwick may possibly get full recognition for the part he played in saving children from Czechoslovakia prior to the Second World War. I saw the need when I was in Prague, just after Christmas 1938. Trevor came out and offered his help and we set up an office together and he agreed to run the Czech side, if, on my return to England, I was able to make workable arrangements with the Home Office. This I was able to do, and my job then was to find suitable families which fulfilled the Home Office conditions of entry. Trevor then went to work and dealt with all the considerable problems at the Prague end and this work he continued to carry

on even when it became more difficult and dangerous when the Germans arrived. He deserves all praise.

* * *

Doreen Warriner spent the start of the war in London, working for the war effort within the Ministry of Economic Welfare and the Political Warfare Executive. She was the first of the BCRC to receive any recognition for their work in Prague, being honoured with an OBE in 1941. She was put forward for this award by her close companion and now friend, Robert Stopford, who stated that a large number of refugees 'owed their lives to her unremitting devotion to their cause … regardless of the risks she herself ran'.[3]

In 1943, Warriner left Britain and headed for the Middle East, where there was more relief work to be carried out. In her capacity as Chief of the United Nations Relief and Rehabilitation Administration food mission in Yugoslavia for the next two years, she helped save countless further lives. Returning to Britain in 1946, she re-joined the University College London (UCL) as a lecturer in the School of Slavonic and East European Studies in 1947. For the next thirteen years, she lectured in the world's leading research centre on Russia, the Baltics, and Central, Eastern and Southeast Europe. In this time, she published many papers, including a diary of her time in Prague from 1938 to 1939, much of which was used to research this book.

In 1965, Warriner was promoted to the role of professor with the UCL, which she continued for seven years. Despite having several love interests through her life, not least during her time in Prague, Warriner never married, instead dedicating her time to her work. She died of a stroke aged 68, in 1972. Like Chadwick, her immense contribution to saving so many Jewish children is still relatively unknown.

* * *

Winton's death on 1 July 2015, aged 106, brought closure to this tripartite rescue mission of Jewish children from Prague. Travelling through Wilson Station in Prague or London Liverpool Street station, you can see statues of Winton in honour of the rescue. Thanks to this story becoming better known, in August 2022, a statue of Trevor Chadwick, carrying a toddler and holding another child's hand, was unveiled next to a children's play area in Swanage, Dorset. Also, a plaque honouring Doreen Warriner has been placed on the side of the Alcron Hotel, where she spent a lot of her time while in Prague.

All of these memorials serve as a reminder that while war brings out the very worst in some, it can also bring out the best in others, not least Winton, Chadwick and Warriner. But they should also honour those children who were left behind and the parents who managed to muster up the courage to put their children on a train, knowing only too well that they would likely never see them again.

Known as 'Winton's children', the 669 infants rescued would go on to achieve amazing things, and today, an estimated 10,000 of their descendants are alive thanks to him and his colleagues. At the time of writing, news broke that one of 'Winton's children', Vera Gissing, had died aged 93 on 12 March 2022. As someone who had campaigned admirably for rescuers to be properly recognised, her death served as a reminder to us all that we have a responsibility to keep this story alive, for the plight of children trapped in war-torn countries is just as relevant today as it was in 1939.

Notes

Chapter 1: Introduction
1. Berlin, Lawrence & Fetzer, Anita, *Dialogue in Politics*, John Benjamins Publishing, 2012, p. 265
2. Ibid.
3. Carr Begbie, Francis, 'The Nicholas Winton Kindertransport Myth Comes Off the Rails', *The Occidental Observer*, 2014
4. *That's Life*, BBC, first broadcast in February 1988
5. Ibid.
6. Ibid.
7. Vallejo, Justin, 'Sir Nicholas Winton: Google Doodle marks birthday of "Britain's Schindler"', *The Independent*, 19 May 2020

Chapter 2: From Wertheim to Winton
1. *Manchester Guardian*, 20 June 1917, https://www.theguardian.com/uk-news/from-the-archive-blog/2017/jul/17/british-royal-family-windsor-name-change-1917
2. Winton, Barbara, *If It's Not Impossible... The Life of Sir Nicholas Winton*, Troubador Publishing, 2014, p. 49
3. Interview with Milenka Jackson, 14 August 1990, https://sounds.bl.uk/related-content/TRANSCRIPTS/021I-C0410X0094XX-ZZZZA0.pdf
4. Ibid.
5. Reeves, Richard, 'A question of character', 31 August 2008, *Prospect Magazine*, https://www.prospectmagazine.co.uk/magazine/aquestionofcharacter
6. Stowe School, The Official Opening of Stanhope House, Stowe School Ltd 2009–2011
7. Nicholas Winton Private Diary, 7 June 1925 and 11 June 1925, Nicholas Winton archive
8. Interview with Milenka Jackson, 14 August 1990, https://sounds.bl.uk/related-content/TRANSCRIPTS/021I-C0410X0094XX-ZZZZA0.pdf
9. Mináč, Matej, *Nicholas Winton's Lottery of Life*, American Friends of the Czech Republic, 2007, p. 141
10. Nicholas Winton Private Diary, 7 June 1925 and 11 June 1925, Nicholas Winton archive
11. Interview with Milenka Jackson, 14 August 1990, https://sounds.bl.uk/related-content/TRANSCRIPTS/021I-C0410X0094XX-ZZZZA0.pdf
12. Ibid.
13. Emanuel, Muriel & Gissing, Vera, *Nicholas Winton and the Rescued Generation*, Vallentine Mitchell, 2002, p. 16

14. Nicholas Winton Private Diary, 7 June 1925 and 11 June 1925, Nicholas Winton archive
15. Ibid.

Chapter 3: Rising from the Ashes

1. Emanuel, Muriel & Gissing, Vera, *Nicholas Winton and the Rescued Generation*, Vallentine Mitchell, 2002, p. 19
2. Goeschel, Christian, *Mussolini and Hitler: The Forging of the Fascist Alliance*, Yale University Press, 2018, New Haven, p. 289
3. Quoted in Roberts, Andrew, *Churchill: Walking With Destiny*, Penguin Random House, 2018, London, pp. 306–307
4. Dubs, Alf, 'Nicholas Winton Saved Me From the Nazis. I Only Found Out 50 Years Later', *The Guardian*, 3 July 2015
5. Hitler, Adolf, *Mein Kampf: My Struggle* (Vols. I & II) (Complete & Illustrated Edition), eKitap Projesi, 2016 (originally from 1939), Chapter 11
6. Longenecker, Bruce W., *Hitler, Jesus, and Our Common Humanity, A Jewish Survivor Interprets Life, History, and the Gospels*, Cascade Books, 2014, p. 44
7. Dubs, Alf, 'Nicholas Winton Saved Me From the Nazis. I Only Found Out 50 Years Later', *The Guardian*, 3 July 2015
8. Interview with Milenka Jackson, 14 August 1990, https://sounds.bl.uk/related-content/TRANSCRIPTS/021I-C0410X0094XX-ZZZZA0.pdf
9. *Gloucestershire Echo*, 9 March 1936
10. Emanuel, Muriel & Gissing, Vera, *Nicholas Winton and the Rescued Generation*, Vallentine Mitchell, 2002, p. 63
11. Nicholas Winton Norwegian Television Interview, 27 April 2014
12. *Montrose, Arbroath and Brechin review; and Forfar and Kincardineshire Advertiser*, 5 August 1938
13. Hitler, Adolf, closing speech at the NSDAP congress in Nuremberg, 1938
14. Knowles, Elizabeth, *Oxford Dictionary of Quotations*, Oxford University Press, 2004, p. 206
15. Churchill, Winston, *The Gathering Storm*, Rosetta Books LLC, 1948, p. 290
16. Radio interview, https://english.radio.cz/sir-nicholas-winton-and-human-cost-peace-our-time-8603793
17. Cazalet, Victor, Grenfell, David, Salter, Arthur & Rathbone, Eleanor, *The Birmingham Daily Post*, 4 January 1939
18. Mináč, Matej, *Children Saved from the Nazis: The Story of Sir Nicholas Winton*, BBC Documentary, 2010
19. Sherman, Ari, *Island Refuge: Britain and Refugees from the Third Reich 1933–1939*, Frank Cass & Co Ltd, 1973, p. 139
20. Cohan, Susan, *Rescue the Perishing. Eleanor Rathbone and the Refugees*, Vallentine Mitchell, 2010, p. 108
21. Smith, Lyn, *Heroes of The Holocaust: Ordinary Britons Who Risked Their Lives To Make A Difference*, Ebury Press, 2013, p. 52
22. Sherman, Ari, *Island Refuge. Britain and Refugees from the Third Reich 1933–1939*, Frank Cass & Co Ltd, 1973, p. 167
23. *Northern Whig*, 9 December 1938

24. Emanuel, Muriel & Gissing, Vera, *Nicholas Winton and the Rescued Generation*, Vallentine Mitchell, 2002, p. 65

Chapter 4: A Different Winter Holiday
1. Interview with Nicholas Winton by Milenka Jackson, 14 August 1990, https://sounds.bl.uk/related-content/TRANSCRIPTS/021I-C0410X0094XX-ZZZZA0.pdf
2. Ibid.
3. Interview with Nicholas Winton from Emanuel, Muriel & Gissing, Vera, *Nicholas Winton and the Rescued Generation*, Vallentine Mitchell, 2002, p. 66
4. Mináč, Matej, *Nicholas Winton's Lottery of Life*, American Friends of the Czech Republic, 2007, p. 75
5. Malvern St James Girls School, www.malvernstjames.co.uk, 2017
6. Gwyer, Barbara, Association of Senior Members, Chronicles 1928–29, St Hugh's College, Oxford, 2015
7. Hastings, Max, *The Secret War: Spies, Codes and Guerrillas 1939–45*, HarperCollins, 2015, p. 2
8. Warriner, Doreen, 'Winter in Prague', *SEER*, Vol. 62, No. 2, 1984
9. Interview with Bill Barazetti from Chadwick, William, *The Rescue of the Prague Refugees*, Troubador Publishing, 2010, p. 91
10. Ibid.
11. Ibid.
12. Ibid.
13. Ibid.
14. Bill Barazetti Obituary, *The Times*, 9 October 2000, https://www.thetimes.co.uk/article/bill-barazetti-hpksql0lfhh
15. Chadwick, William, *The Rescue of the Prague Refugees*, Troubador Publishing, 2010, p. 91
16. Emanuel, Muriel & Gissing, Vera, *Nicholas Winton and the Rescued Generation*, Vallentine Mitchell, 2002, p. 105
17. Chadwick, William, *The Rescue of the Prague Refugees*, Troubador Publishing, 2010, p. 91
18. Nicholas Winton archive, 1 January 1939
19. Interview with Nicholas Winton from Emanuel, Muriel & Gissing, Vera, *Nicholas Winton and the Rescued Generation*, Vallentine Mitchell, 2002, p. 66
20. Norwegian Television Interview, 27 April 2014
21. Winton, Barbara, *If It's Not Impossible… The Life of Sir Nicholas Winton*, Troubador Publishing, 2014, p. 17
22. Emanuel, Muriel & Gissing, Vera, *Nicholas Winton and the Rescued Generation*, Vallentine Mitchell, 2002, p. 71
23. Winton, Barbara, *If It's Not Impossible… The Life of Sir Nicholas Winton*, Troubador Publishing, 2014, p. 20
24. Chadwick, William, *The Rescue of the Prague Refugees*, Troubador Publishing, 2010, p. 41
25. Nicholas Winton archive, 14 January 1939
26. Interview with Nicholas Winton from Emanuel, Muriel & Gissing, Vera, *Nicholas Winton and the Rescued Generation*, Vallentine Mitchell, 2002, p. 68

27. Winton, Barbara, *If It's Not Impossible… The Life of Sir Nicholas Winton*, Troubador Publishing, 2014, p. 18
28. Interview with Ben Abeles from 'Children Saved from the Nazis: The Story of Sir Nicholas Winton', 18 May 2017, https://www.youtube.com/watch?v=nT0yPjj0UqQ
29. Chadwick, William, *The Rescue of the Prague Refugees*, Troubador Publishing, 2010, p. 40
30. Winton, Barbara, *If It's Not Impossible… The Life of Sir Nicholas Winton*, Troubador Publishing, 2014, p. 19
31. Ibid.

Chapter 5: Sightseeing
1. Nicholas Winton archive, 14 January 1939
2. Winton, Barbara, *If It's Not Impossible… The Life of Sir Nicholas Winton*, Troubador Publishing, 2014, p. 23
3. Ibid.
4. Cohan, Susan, *Rescue the Perishing: Eleanor Rathbone and the Refugees*, Vallentine Mitchell, 2010, p. 116
5. Ibid.
6. Letter to Barbara Winton, 14 January 1939, Nicholas Winton archive
7. Warriner, Doreen from Warriner, Henry, *Doreen Warriner's War*, The Book Guild, 2019, London, p. 43
8. Warriner, Doreen, 'Winter in Prague', *SEER*, Vol. 62, No. 2, 1984, p. 218
9. Ibid.
10. Letter to Barbara Winton, Nicholas Winton archive, 14 January 1939
11. Chadwick, William, *The Rescue of the Prague Refugees*, Troubador Publishing, 2010, p. 40
12. Warriner, Henry, *Doreen Warriner's War*, The Book Guild, 2019, London, p. 43
13. Winton, Barbara, *If It's Not Impossible… The Life of Sir Nicholas Winton*, Troubador Publishing, 2014, p. 20
14. Mináč, Matej, *Nicholas Winton's Lottery of Life*, American Friends of the Czech Republic, 2007, p. 141
15. Ibid. p. 125

Chapter 6: Then There Were Three
1. Chadwick, William, *The Rescue of the Prague Refugees*, Troubador Publishing, 2010, p. 70
2. Bourne, Peter, www.dragonschool.org, The Dragon School Trust, 2017
3. Phelps, Guy, 'Forgotten Heroes of the Kindertransport', *The Guardian*, 3 July 2017
4. Annual Colonial Reports, Nigeria Report for 1930, His Majesty's Stationary Office, 1931, p. 7
5. Chadwick, William, *The Rescue of the Prague Refugees*, Troubador Publishing, 2010, p. 70
6. Chadwick, Trevor, from Gershon, Karen, *We Came as Children: A Collective Autobiography of Refugees*, Victor Gollancz, 1966, p. 22
7. Ibid.

8. Interview with Nicholas Winton from Mináč, Matej, *Nicholas Winton's Lottery of Life*, American Friends of the Czech Republic, 2007, p. 86
9. Emanuel, Muriel & Gissing, Vera, *Nicholas Winton and the Rescued Generation*, Vallentine Mitchell, 2002, p. 102
10. Winton, Nick, 'From Stockbroker to Hero: The Story of Sir Nicholas Winton', Holocaust Memorial Centre, 19 July 2019
11. Ibid.
12. Interview with Nicholas Winton from 'Children Saved from the Nazis: The Story of Sir Nicholas Winton', 18 May 2017
13. Letter to Barbara Winton, Winton, Barbara, *If It's Not Impossible... The Life of Sir Nicholas Winton*, Troubador Publishing, 2014, p. 24
14. Letter from Doreen Warriner to Margaret Layton, Emanuel, Muriel & Gissing, Vera, *Nicholas Winton and the Rescued Generation*, Vallentine Mitchell, 2002, p. 72
15. Winton, Nick, 'From Stockbroker to Hero: The Story of Sir Nicholas Winton', Holocaust Memorial Centre, 19 July 2019
16. Winton, Nicholas, 'What Makes a Hero? A letter from Nicholas Winton', Holocaust Education Trust, 28 March 1999
17. Interview with Nicholas Winton from CBC News: *The National*, 2 July 2015
18. Chadwick, Trevor, from Gershon, Karen, *We Came as Children: A Collective Autobiography of Refugees*, Victor Gollancz, 1966, p. 22
19. Ibid.
20. Warriner, Doreen, 'Winter in Prague', *SEER*, Vol. 62, No. 2, 1984, p. 223
21. Warriner, Henry, *Doreen Warriner's War*, The Book Guild, 2019, London, p. 65
22. Chadwick, Trevor, from Gershon, Karen, *We Came as Children: A Collective Autobiography of Refugees*, Victor Gollancz, 1966, p. 22
23. Winton, Barbara, *If It's Not Impossible... The Life of Sir Nicholas Winton*, Troubador Publishing, 2014, p. 27
24. Letter by Nicholas Winton, 4 May 1939, ibid., p.33
25. Winton, Barbara, *If It's Not Impossible... The Life of Sir Nicholas Winton*, Troubador Publishing, 2014, p. 35
26. *South Wales Evening Post*, 20 April 1939
27. Mináč, Matej, *Nicholas Winton's Lottery of Life*, American Friends of the Czech Republic, 2007, p. 85
28. Chadwick, Trevor, from Gershon, Karen, *We Came as Children: A Collective Autobiography of Refugees*, Victor Gollancz, 1966, p. 23
29. Mináč, Matej, *Nicholas Winton's Lottery of Life*, American Friends of the Czech Republic, 2007, p. 106.
30. Ibid., p.103
31. Winton, Nick, 'From Stockbroker to Hero: The Story of Sir Nicholas Winton', Holocaust Memorial Centre, 19 July 2019
32. Chadwick, Trevor, from Gershon, Karen, *We Came as Children: A Collective Autobiography of Refugees*, Victor Gollancz, 1966, p. 22
33. Interview with Nicholas Winton from Norwegian Television, 27 April 2014
34. Ibid.

Chapter 7: Occupation

1. Warriner, Doreen, 'Winter in Prague', *SEER*, Vol. 62, No. 2, 1984, p. 224
2. Mináč, Matej, *Nicholas Winton's Lottery of Life*, American Friends of the Czech Republic, 2007, p.38
3. Ibid.
4. Hastings, Max, *The Secret War: Spies, Codes and Guerrillas 1939–45*, HarperCollins, 2015, p. 2
5. Mináč, Matej, *Nicholas Winton's Lottery of Life*, American Friends of the Czech Republic, 2007, p. 80
6. Chadwick, Trevor, from Gershon, Karen, *We Came as Children: A Collective Autobiography of Refugees*, Victor Gollancz, 1966, p. 24
7. Interview with Nicholas Winton from Mináč, Matej, *Nicholas Winton's Lottery of Life*, American Friends of the Czech Republic, 2007, p. 110
8. Warriner, Doreen, 'Winter in Prague', *SEER*, Vol. 62, No. 2, 1984, p. 234
9. Winton, Nicholas, 'What Makes a Hero? A letter from Nicholas Winton', Holocaust Education Trust, 28 March 1999
10. Winton, Barbara, *If It's Not Impossible... The Life of Sir Nicholas Winton*, Troubador Publishing, 2014, p. 29
11. Ibid.
12. Ibid.
13. Chadwick, Trevor, from Gershon, Karen, *We came as Childre: A Collective Autobiography of Refugees*, Victor Gollancz, 1966, p. 23
14. Emanuel, Muriel & Gissing, Vera, *Nicholas Winton and the Rescued Generation*, Vallentine Mitchell, 2002, p. 102
15. *Newcastle Evening Chronicle*, 14 August 1939
16. Chadwick, Trevor, from Gershon, Karen, *We Came as Children: A Collective Autobiography of Refugees*, Victor Gollancz, 1966, p. 23
17. Ibid.
18. Interview with Nicholas Winton from Emanuel, Muriel & Gissing, Vera, *Nicholas Winton and the Rescued Generation*, Vallentine Mitchell, 2002, p. 94

Chapter 8: 23:00 From Wilson Station

1. Mináč, Matej, *Nicholas Winton's Lottery of Life*, American Friends of the Czech Republic, 2007, p. 104
2. Ibid.
3. Chadwick, Trevor, from Gershon, Karen, *We Came as Children: A Collective Autobiography of Refugees*, Victor Gollancz, 1966, p. 24
4. Ibid., p. 26
5. Warriner, Doreen, 'Winter in Prague', *SEER*, Vol. 62, No. 2, 1984, p. 234
6. Gershon, Karen, *We Came as Children: A Collective Autobiography of Refugees*, Victor Gollancz, 1966, p. 26
7. Mináč, Matej, *Nicholas Winton's Lottery of Life*, American Friends of the Czech Republic, 2007, p. 104
8. Chadwick, Trevor, from Gershon, Karen, *We Came as Children: A Collective Autobiography of Refugees*, Victor Gollancz, 1966, p. 24
9. Gershon, Karen, *We Came as Children: A Collective Autobiography of Refugees*, Victor Gollancz, 1966, p. 26

10. Mináč, Matej, *Nicholas Winton's Lottery of Life*, American Friends of the Czech Republic, 2007, p. 109
11. Winton, Barbara, *If It's Not Impossible... The Life of Sir Nicholas Winton*, Troubador Publishing, 2014, p. 29
12. Gershon, Karen, *We Came as Children: A Collective Autobiography of Refugees*, Victor Gollancz, 1966, p. 29
13. Emanuel, Muriel & Gissing, Vera, *Nicholas Winton and the Rescued Generation*, Vallentine Mitchell, 2002, p. 118
14. Warriner, Henry, *Doreen Warriner's War*, The Book Guild, 2019, London, p. 77
15. Chadwick, Trevor, from Gershon, Karen, *We Came as Children: A Collective Autobiography of Refugees*, Victor Gollancz, 1966, p. 24
16. Ibid.
17. Mináč, Matej, *Nicholas Winton's Lottery of Life*, American Friends of the Czech Republic, 2007, pp. 90–1
18. Chadwick, Trevor, from Gershon, Karen, *We Came as Children: A Collective Autobiography of Refugees*, Victor Gollancz, 1966, p. 23
19. Stopford, Robert, Private Papers, p. 39
20. Winton, Nick, 'From Stockbroker to Hero: The Story of Sir Nicholas Winton', Holocaust Memorial Centre, 19 July 2019
21. Chadwick, Trevor, from Gershon, Karen, *We Came as Children: A Collective Autobiography of Refugees*, Victor Gollancz, 1966, p. 24
22. Gershon, Karen, *We Came as Children: A Collective Autobiography of Refugees*, Victor Gollancz, 1966, p. 26
23. Ibid.
24. Winton, Barbara, *If It's Not Impossible... The Life of Sir Nicholas Winton*, Troubador Publishing, 2014, p. 30
25. Gershon, Karen, *We Came as Children: A Collective Autobiography of Refugees*, Victor Gollancz, 1966, p. 28
26. Chadwick, William, *The Rescue of the Prague Refugees*, Troubador Publishing, 2010, p. 83
27. Gershon, Karen, *We Came as Children: A Collective Autobiography of Refugees*, Victor Gollancz, 1966, p. 24
28. Ibid.
29. Chadwick, William, *The Rescue of the Prague Refugees*, Troubador Publishing, 2010, p. 79
30. Winton, Nicholas, 'What Makes a Hero? A letter from Nicholas Winton', Holocaust Education Trust, 28 March 1999
31. Mináč, Matej, *Nicholas Winton's Lottery of Life*, American Friends of the Czech Republic, 2007, p. 225
32. Ibid., p. 210
33. Holocaust Memorial Day Trust, Vera Lowyova MBE, https://www.hmd.org.uk/resource/hmd-2016-vera-schaufeld/
34. Winton, Nick, 'From Stockbroker to Hero: The Story of Sir Nicholas Winton', Holocaust Memorial Centre, 19 July 2019
35. Holocaust Memorial Day Trust, Vera Lowyova MBE, https://www.hmd.org.uk/resource/hmd-2016-vera-schaufeld/
36. Ibid.

37. Holocaust Memorial Group, Hartlepool, 26 January 2016
38. Mináč, Matej, *Nicholas Winton's Lottery of Life*, American Friends of the Czech Republic, 2007, p. 189
39. Ibid., p. 219.
40. Ibid., p.128
41. Soames, Mary, *Speaking for Themselves: The Personal Letters of Winston and Clementine Churchill*, Transworld Publishers, 1998, London, p. 541

Chapter 9: The Duration

1. *The Guardian*, 6 August 2009, https://www.theguardian.com/world/2009/sep/06/second-world-war-declaration-chamberlain
2. Norwegian Television Interview, 27 April 2014
3. Ibid.
4. Warriner, Henry, *Doreen Warriner's War*, The Book Guild, 2019, London, p. 89.
5. Winton, Barbara, *If It's Not Impossible... The Life of Sir Nicholas Winton*, Troubador Publishing, 2014, p. 123
6. Kramer, Ann, *Conscientious Objectors of the First World War: A Determined Resistance*, Pen & Sword, 2014, Barnsley, p. 1
7. Warriner, Henry, *Doreen Warriner's War*, The Book Guild, 2019, London, p. 105.
8. Nicholas Winton archive, Red Cross Papers, April–May 1940
9. Ibid., Red Cross Certificate
10. Winton, Barbara, *If It's Not Impossible... The Life of Sir Nicholas Winton*, Troubador Publishing, 2014, p. 125
11. *Nottingham Journal*, 16 March 1940
12. Nicholas Winton archive, Red Cross Papers, April–May 1940
13. Ibid.
14. Winton, Barbara, *If It's Not Impossible... The Life of Sir Nicholas Winton*, Troubador Publishing, 2014, p. 127
15. Nicholas Winton archive, Red Cross Papers, April–May 1940
16. Ramsey, L.F., 'Battle of Britain over West Wittering', from the *West Wittering Women's Institute Village Scrapbook*, http://www2.westsussex.gov.uk/learning-resources/LR/battle_of_britain_over_west_wittering_bookcf09.pdf?docid=f5f49180-2547-4d51-9b34-ded3c5ca78aa&version=-1
17. *Mid-Sussex Times*, 11 March 1941
18. Nicholas Winton archive, Red Cross Papers, April–May 1940
19. Winton, Barbara, *If It's Not Impossible... The Life of Sir Nicholas Winton*, Troubador Publishing, 2014, p. 130
20. Roberts, Andrew, *Churchill: Walking With Destiny*, Penguin Random House, 2018, London, p. 529
21. RAF Recruitment Brochure from https://kenfentonswar.com/raf-training/
22. Roberts, Andrew, *Churchill: Walking With Destiny*, Penguin Random House, 2018, London, p. 584
23. RAF Recruitment Brochure from https://kenfentonswar.com/raf-training/
24. *The Courier and Advertiser*, 6 June 1938
25. Winton, Barbara, *If It's Not Impossible... The Life of Sir Nicholas Winton*, Troubador Publishing, 2014, p. 135

26. *Illustrated London News*, 20 August 1938
27. Nicholas Winton archive, Red Cross Papers, November 1945
28. Ibid., 29 November 1944
29. Winton, Barbara, *If It's Not Impossible... The Life of Sir Nicholas Winton*, Troubador Publishing, 2014, p. 142
30. Nicholas Winton archive, Red Cross Papers, 29 November 1944

Chapter 10: Peacetime
1. *Manchester Evening News*, 17 August 1944
2. Warriner, Henry, *Doreen Warriner's War*, The Book Guild, 2019, London, p. 106.
3. Winton, Barbara, *If It's Not Impossible... The Life of Sir Nicholas Winton*, Troubador Publishing, 2014, p. 173
4. Mináč, Matej, *Nicholas Winton's Lottery of Life*, American Friends of the Czech Republic, 2007, p. 128
5. *The Scotsman*, 12 September 1946
6. Winton, Barbara, *If It's Not Impossible... The Life of Sir Nicholas Winton*, Troubador Publishing, 2014, p. 172
7. Warriner, Henry, *Doreen Warriner's War*, The Book Guild, 2019, London, p. 101.
8. Marshall, Katherine, *The World Bank: From Reconstruction to Development to Equity*, Taylor & Francis, 2008, London, p. 1
9. *Leicester Evening Mail*, 11 September 1947
10. Steil, Benn, *The Marshall Plan: Dawn of the Cold War*, Oxford University Press, 2018, p. 12.
11. Winton, Barbara, *If It's Not Impossible... The Life of Sir Nicholas Winton*, Troubador Publishing, 2014, p. 176
12. Winton, Barbara, *If It's Not Impossible... The Life of Sir Nicholas Winton*, Troubador Publishing, 2014, p. 177
13. Norwegian Television Interview, 27 April 2014
14. Nicholas Winton archive, 24 January 1950
15. Norwegian Television Interview, 27 April 2014
16. Winton, Barbara, *If It's Not Impossible... The Life of Sir Nicholas Winton*, Troubador Publishing, 2014, p. 207
17. https://abbeyfieldmaidenhead.org.uk/about-us/history/
18. *Sunday Mirror*, 28 February 1988
19. CBC News: *The National*, 2 July 2015
20. Winton, Barbara, *If It's Not Impossible... The Life of Sir Nicholas Winton*, Troubador Publishing, 2014, p. 191
21. BBC, 29 June 2009, http://news.bbc.co.uk/1/hi/england/berkshire/8125546.stm

Epilogue
1. Carr Begbie, Francis, 'The Nicholas Winton Kindertransport Myth Comes off the Rails', *The Observer*, 2014
2. Warriner, Henry, *Doreen Warriner's War*, The Book Guild, 2019, London, p. 94
3. Chadwick, William, *The Rescue of the Prague Refugees*, Troubador Publishing, 2010, p. 36

List of Acronyms

ARP	Air Raid Precautions
BCRC	British Committee for Refugees from Czechoslovakia
CIA	Central Intelligence Agency
IBRD	International Bank for Reconstruction and Development
KSČ	Communist Party of Czechoslovakia
MCCG	Movement for the Care of Children from Germany
NCCL	National Council for Civil Liberties
PCR	Parliamentary Committee on Refugees
PhD	Doctor of Philosophy
RAF	Royal Air Force
RMS	Royal Mail Ship
SdP	Sudeten German Party
SIS	Secret Intelligence Service
SSD	Sudeten Social Democratic Party
UCL	University College London
UCS	University College School

Bibliography and Sources

Abel Smith, Edward, *Active Goodness: The True Story of How Trevor Chadwick, Doreen Warriner & Nicolas Winton Rescued Thousands From The Nazis*, Kwill Books, 2017, London

Albright, Madeleine, *Prague Winter: A Personal Story of Remembrance and War, 1937–1948*, HarperPerennial, 2013, New York

Bachstein, Martin, *Wenzel Jaksch und die Sudetendeutsche Sozialdemokratie*, R. Oldenbourg, 1974, Prague

Bader, Marie, *Life and Love in Nazi Prague: Letters from an Occupied City*, Bloomsbury Academic, 2019, London

Bailey, Brenda, *A Quaker Couple in Nazi Germany: Leonhard Friedrich Survives Buchenwald*, Sessions, 1994, London

Bailey, Brenda, 'The Integrity of German Friends During the Twelve Years of Nazi Rule', https://quaker.org/legacy/minnfm/peace/integrity_of_german_friends_duri.htm

Balint, Benjamin, *Kafka's Last Trial, The Strange Case of a Literary Legacy*, Picador, 2018, London

Brade, Laura E. & Holmes, Rose, 'Troublesome Sainthood: Nicholas Winton and the Contested History of Child Rescue in Prague, 1938–1940', from *History & Memory*, Vol. 29, No. 1, Spring/Summer 2017, pp. 3–40, Indiana University Press, 2017, Bloomington

Brown, Martin D., 'A Munich Winter or a Prague Spring? The evolution of British policy towards the Sudeten Germans from October 1938 to September 1939', http://www.academia.edu

Bryant, Chad, *Prague in Black: Nazi Rule and Czech Nationalism*, Harvard University Press, 2007, Massachusetts

Chadwick, William, *The Rescue of the Prague Refugees*, Troubador Publishing, 2010

Cohan, Susan, 'A British Woman's Mission Abroad: Doreen Warriner and the British Committee for Refugees from Czechoslovakia', University of Southampton, https://www.yumpu.com/en/document/read/12047578/pdf-a-british-womans-mission-abroad-united-academics

Cohan, Susan, *Rescue the Perishing: Eleanor Rathbone and the Refugees*, Vallentine Mitchell, 2010

Cohan, Susan, 'Voluntary Refugee Work in Britain, 1933–39: An Overview', https://publishup.uni-potsdam.de/opus4-ubp/frontdoor/deliver/index/docId/5929/file/pardes18_s21_34.pdf

Demetz, Peter, *Prague in Danger: The Years of German Occupation, 1939–45: Memories and History, Terror and Resistance, Theater and Jazz, Film and Poetry, Politics and War*, Farrar, Straus and Giroux, 2009, New York

Edelman, Marek, *The Ghetto Fights, Warsaw 1943–45*, Bookmarks, 1990, London
Eisen, Norman, *The Last Palace, Europe's Turbulent Century in Five Lives and One Legendary House*, Crown Publishing Group, 2018, New York
Emanuel, Muriel & Gissing, Vera, *Nicholas Winton and the Rescued Generation*, Vallentine Mitchell, 2002
Faber, David, *Munich, 1938: Appeasement and World War II*, Simon & Schuster, 2008, New York
Fast, Vera K., *Children's Exodus: A History of the Kindertransport*, I.B. Tauris, 2011, London
Garrett, Patrick, *Of Fortunes and War: Clare Hollingworth, first of the female war correspondents*, Thistle Publishing, 2016, London
Gershon, Karen, *We Came as Children: A Collective Autobiography of Refugees*, Victor Gollancz, 1966, London
Goeschel, Christian, *Mussolini and Hitler: The Forging of the Fascist Alliance*, Yale University Press, 2018, New Haven
Hollingworth, Clare, *Front Line*, Jonathan Cape, 1990, London
Holmes, Rose, 'A Moral Business: British Quaker work with Refugees from Fascism, 1933–39', thesis submitted for the degree of Doctor of Philosophy, University of Sussex, 2013
Hubback, David, *No Ordinary Press Baron: A Life of Walter Layton*, Weidenfeld & Nicolson, 1985, London
Jaksch, Wenzel, 'Farewell to Bohemia', www.radio.cz, 2011
Jaksch, Wenzel & Kolarz, Walter, *England and the Last Free Germans, The Story of a Rescue*, Lincolns-Prager, 1941, London
Joukowsky, Artemis, *Defying the Nazis: The Sharps' War*, Beacon Press, 2016, Boston
Kramer, Ann, *Conscientious Objectors of the First World War: A Determined Resistance*, Pen & Sword, 2014, Barnsley
Lerski, Jerzy Jan, *Historical Dictionary of Poland, 966–1945*, Greenwood Publishing Group, 1996
Leverton, Bertha & Lowensohn, Shmuel, *I Came Alone: The Stories of the Kindertransports*, Book Guild Publishing, 2005, London
Longenecker, Bruce W., *Hitler, Jesus, and Our Common Humanity: A Jewish Survivor Interprets Life, History, and the Gospels*, Cascade Books, 2014
Lukes, Igor, *Czechoslovakia between Stalin and Hitler: The Diplomacy of Edvard Beneš in the 1930s*, Oxford University Press, 1996, Oxford
Marshall, Katherine, *The World Bank: From Reconstruction to Development to Equity*, Taylor & Francis, London, 2008
Martin, Nikolaus, *Prague Winter*, Peter Halban Publishers, 1990, London
McDonough, Frank, *The Gestapo: The Myth and Reality of Hitler's Secret Police*, Coronet, 2015
Mináč, Matej, *Nicholas Winton's Lottery of Life*, American Friends of the Czech Republic, 2007
Moos, Merilyn, *Breaking the Silence: Voices of the British Children of Refugees from Nazism*, Rowman & Littlefield International, 2015, London
Neiberg, Michael S., *The World War I Reader*, New York University Press, 2007, New York

Oldfield, Sybil, "'It Is Usually She': The Role of British Women in the Rescue and Care of the Kindertransport Kinder', *Shofar*, Vol. 23, No. 1, 2004, pp. 57–70
Oldfield, Sybil, *Women Humanitarians: A Biographical Dictionary of British Women Active between 1900 and 1950*, Bloomsbury, 2001, New York
Oppenheimer, Deborah, *Into the Arms of Strangers: Stories of the Kindertransport*, Bloomsbury, 2017, London
Paldiel, Mordecai, *Saving One's Own: Jewish Rescuers during the Holocaust*, University of Nebraska Press, 2017, Lincoln, NE
Pedersen, Susan, *Eleanor Rathbone and the Politics of Conscience*, Yale University Press, 2004, New Haven
Reed, Douglas, *Disgrace Abounding*, Jonathan Cape, 1939, London
Roberts, Andrew, *Churchill: Walking With Destiny*, Penguin Random House, 2018, London
Seymour, Miranda, *Noble Endeavours: The Life of Two Countries, England and Germany, In Many Stories*, Simon & Schuster, 2013, London
Sharp Cogan, Martha, *Church Mouse in The White House*, Journey to Freedom LLC, 2016, New York
Sharp, Waitstill, *The Liberation of The Human Spirit*, Journey to Freedom LLC, 2016, New York
Shepherd, Naomi, *A Refuge from Darkness: Wilfrid Israel and the Rescue of the Jews*, Pantheon Books, 1984, Germany
Shepherd, Naomi, *Wilfrid Israel: German Jewry's Secret Ambassador*, Littlehampton Book Services, 1984, London
Sherman, Ari, *Island Refuge: Britain and Refugees from the Third Reich 1933–1939*, Frank Cass & Co, 1973
Smetana, Vít, *In the Shadow of Munich: British Policy towards Czechoslovakia from 1938 to 1942*, Karolinum Press, 2008, Prague
Smith, Lyn, *Heroes of the Holocaust: Ordinary Britons Who Risked Their Lives to Make a Difference*, Ebury Press, 2013, London
Sniegon, Tomas, *Vanished History: The Holocaust in Czech and Slovak Historical Culture*, Berghahn Books, 2014, New York
Soames, Mary, *Speaking for Themselves: The Personal Letters of Winston and Clementine Churchill*, Transworld Publishers, 1998, London
Steil, Benn, *The Marshall Plan: Dawn of the Cold War*, Oxford University Press, 2018
Stocks, Mary D., *Eleanor Rathbone: A Biography*, Victor Gollancz, 1949, London
Strange, Joan, *Despatches From the Home Front: The War Diaries of Joan Strange 1939–1945*, self-published, 2013
Subak, Susan Elisabeth, *Rescue and Flight: American Relief Workers Who Defied the Nazis*, University of Nebraska Press, 2010, Lincoln, NE
Tombs, Isabelle, 'The Victory of Socialist "Vansittartism": Labour and the German Question, 1941–5', from *20th Century British History*, Vol. 7, Iss. 3, 1996
Turner, Barry, *… And the Policeman Smiled: 10,000 Children Escape from Nazi Europe*, Bloomsbury, 1990, London
Warriner, Doreen, 'Winter in Prague', *The Slavonic and East European Review*, Vol. 62, No. 2, 1984
Warriner, Henry, *Doreen Warriner's War*, The Book Guild, 2019, London

Weisskopf, Kurt, *The Agony of Czechoslovakia '38/'39*, Elek Books, 1968, London
Williams, Bill, 'Serious Concern: Manchester Quakers and Refugees, 1938–40', University Press Scholarship Online, http://www.kindertransport.info/concern.html
Winton, Barbara, *If It's Not Impossible... The Life of Sir Nicholas Winton*, Troubador Publishing, 2014, London

Quoted interviews
Documentary by Mináč, Matej, *Children Saved from the Nazis: The Story of Sir Nicholas Winton*, BBC, 2010
Interview with Ben Abeles from *Children Saved from the Nazis: The Story of Sir Nicholas Winton*, 18 May 2017, https://www.youtube.com/watch?v=nT0yPjj0UqQ
Interview with Milenka Jackson, 14 August 1990, https://sounds.bl.uk/related-content/TRANSCRIPTS/021I-C0410X0094XX-ZZZZA0.pdf
Interview with Nicholas Winton from CBC News: *The National*, 2 July 2015
Norwegian Television, 'Sir Nicolas Winton Interview', 27 April 2014
Radio Prague, 'Sir Nicholas Winton and the human cost of "peace for our time"', https://english.radio.cz/sir-nicholas-winton-and-human-cost-peace-our-time-8603793
Talk by Winton, Nick, 'From Stockbroker to Hero: The Story of Sir Nicholas Winton', Holocaust Memorial Centre, 19 July 2019

Archives
National Archives, Kew
Society of Friends House, London
Imperial War Museum, London
Nicolas Winton Private Archives
Holocaust Memorial Centre, London

Quoted News Sources
'Bill Barazetti Obituary', *The Times*, 9 October 2000
'British Royal Family Windsor Name Change', *Manchester Guardian*, 20 June 1917, https://www.theguardian.com/uk-news/from-the-archive-blog/2017/jul/17/british-royal-family-windsor-name-change-1917
'Earl Baldwin Fund', *Northern Whig*, 9 December 1938
'Evian Conference', *Montrose, Arbroath and Brechin Review; and Forfar and Kincardineshire Advertiser*, 5 August 1938
'Incoming War', *Gloucestershire Echo*, 9 March 1936
That's Life, BBC, first broadcast in February 1988, https://www.bbc.co.uk/archive/nicholas_winton_on_thats_life/zbmxhbk
Dubs, Alf, 'Nicholas Winton Saved Me From the Nazis. I Only Found Out 50 Years Later', *The Guardian*, 3 July 2015
Phelps, Guy, 'Forgotten Heroes of the Kindertransport', *The Guardian*, 3 July 2017
Lee, Reverend Rosaland, *South Wales Evening Post*, 20 April 1939
Reeves, Richard, 'A question of character', 31 August 2008, *Prospect Magazine*, https://www.prospectmagazine.co.uk/magazine/aquestionofcharacter
Vallejo, Justin, 'Sir Nicholas Winton: Google Doodle marks birthday of "Britain's Schindler"', *The Independent*, 19 May 2020

Vera Lowyova MBE, Holocaust Memorial Day Trust
Fleischmann, Milena, Holocaust Memorial Group, Hartlepool, 26 January 2016
'Second World War Declaration', *The Guardian*, 6 September 2009
'Royal Interest In Ambulance Unit', *Nottingham Journal*, 16 March 1940
Ramsey, L.F., 'Battle of Britain over West Wittering', *The West Wittering Women's Institute Village Scrapbook*
'Weekend Blitz on London', *Mid-Sussex Times*, 11 March 1941
'Link Trainer', *Illustrated London News*, 20 August 1938
'International Committee for Refugees in London', *Manchester Evening News*, 17 August 1944
'Nazi Reparations', *The Scotsman*, 12 September 1946
'International Bank for Reconstruction and Development', *Leicester Evening Mail*, 11 September 1947
'The Lost Children. Little Refugees Left Waiting For Their Brave Pied Piper', *Sunday Mirror*, 28 February 1988
"UK Schindler' in birthday flight', BBC, 29 June 2009

Index

A.E. Wassermann, 20
Abbeyfield, 133
Abbeyfield Society, 133
Abeles, Ben, 56
Abingdon, 132
Air Raid Precaution (ARP), 112, 117
Aitken, Max (Lord Beaverbrook), 118
Alcron Hotel, 43, 88, 93, 138
Alsace-Lorraine, 21
Altwood Bailey, 131
Anschluss, 25, 27
Ant and Dec, 4
Archbishop of Canterbury, 3
Archduke Franz Ferdinand of Austria, 8
Armistice, 6
Auschwitz, 108
Austria, 8, 21, 25, 26, 27, 29, 35, 36, 37, 55, 71, 75, 78
Austro-Hungarian Empire, 8, 28
Axis Powers, 119

Baldwin, Stanley, 36
Baldwin Fund, 36, 79
Baltics, 137
Barazetti, Anna, 48–50
Barazetti, Bill:
  birth, 47
  early life, 48
  education, 48
  spying, 48–50
  marriage, 49
  birth of son, 50
  work, 48, 50
  teaching Winton Czech, 56
Barbican Mission, 64, 66
Barbour, Jean, 102

Battle, East Sussex, 69
Battle of Britain, 103, 115, 116
BBC, 3
Beer Hall Putsch, 20
Behrens, George Eduard, 15–16
Belgium, 21, 119
Beneš, Edvard, 30, 31
Bennett, Arnold, 59
Bentham, Jeremy, 9
Beran, Rudolf, 84–5
Blake, Martin:
  career, 38
  decision to travel to Prague, 38–9
  refugee work, 45, 47
  concern about child refugees, 51
  children's section of the BCRC, 51–2, 76
  return to Britain, 52
  reunion in Prague, 126
Blitz, 115–16
Bohemian Kingdom, 28
Bömelburg, Karl, 89, 90, 91, 92, 99, 100, 101
Book of Common Prayer, The, 13
Boulogne, 114
Bourne, Peter, 67
Brasier, Theresa *see* May, Theresa
British Air Ministry, 120
British Committee for Refugees from Czechoslovakia (BCRC), 47, 50, 51, 54, 55, 58–63, 66, 69–70, 72–9, 82, 83, 85, 88, 91–3, 97, 101, 106, 110, 122, 126, 135, 137
British Expeditionary Force, 113
British Home Office, 53, 78, 79, 82, 98, 136

British Labour Party, 22, 44, 46–7, 49, 133
British Secret Intelligence Service (MI6), 88
British Union of Fascists, 14
Brown, Bob, 70
Brown, Capability, 10
Brussels, 120
Buckingham Palace, 113, 133
Bundesregierung, 22–3

Calais, 114–15
Cambridge, 11, 38
Caribbean, 42
Central British Fund for World Jewish Relief, 36
Central Hall Westminster, 2
Central Intelligence Agency (CIA), 127
Chadwick, Hugh, 69
Chadwick, Marjorie, 69, 70, 136
Chadwick, R.M., 67, 71
Chadwick, Trevor:
   early life, 66–7
   education, 67–8
   relationship with Nicholas Winton, 66, 68, 71, 72
   working for the Colonial Service, 68–9
   relationship with Marjorie, 69, 71, 136
   teaching at Forres School, 69–70
   eccentricities, 70
   arrival in Prague, 66
   meeting Doreen Warriner, 66, 71
   working for the BCRC, 72
   meeting families, 72–3, 93
   return flight to England, 75
   first air rescue, 75
   second air rescue, 76–7, 80
   third air rescue, 77
   putting chosen children on standby, 82–3
   expanding remit with the BCRC, 83
   negotiating with the Gestapo, 90–2, 99, 100
   first train rescue, 85–7
   second train rescue, 95–8
   third train rescue, 98–100
   fourth train rescue, 100–101
   departure from Czechoslovakia, 101
   spying, 101–102
   joining the Royal Navy Reserve, 135
   joining the RAF, 135–6
   dismissal from the RAF, 136
   second marriage and divorce, 136
   contraction of tuberculosis, 136
   third marriage to Sigi, 136
   death, 136
   posthumous recognition, 136–7, 138
Chadwick, William, 67, 101
Chamberlain, Neville, 31, 34, 35
Chancellor of the Exchequer, 34, 127
China, 103
Church of England, 6–7, 67
Churchill, Clementine, 109
Churchill, Winston, 22, 32, 47, 109
Cold War, 126
Colonial Service, 68, 69
Communist Party of Czechoslovakia, 126
Cordon Bleu, 129
Courier and Advertiser, 118
Crédit National, 127
Crews & Company, 20, 52, 112
Cricklewood, 107
Culpin, Ewart Gladstone, 62
Cumbria, 67
Czech Intelligence Office, 49
Czech Republic, 1, 2, 4, 8, 14, 21, 25, 28, 29, 30, 31, 32, 33, 34, 37, 38, 40, 42, 43, 45, 46, 47, 48, 49, 50, 52, 56, 62, 71, 74, 75, 76, 77, 80, 83, 84, 85, 86, 87, 88, 89, 94, 96, 98, 99, 101, 102, 104, 105, 108, 109, 111, 122, 126, 136
Czech Secret Police, 48
Czechoslovakia *see* Czech Republic

Daily Telegraph, 61
Dalton, Hugh, 127
Danzig, 21
de Havilland, Geoffrey, 119
Denmark, 21, 127, 129
Der Stürmer, 57
Dodbrook House, 131
Dolná Krupá Castle, 33
Dorset, 138

Dowding, Hugh, 118
Dragon (club), 18
Dragon School, 18, 67
Dubs, Alf, 22, 24
Dunkirk, 113, 114

Earl Baldwin Fund, 36
Eberstadt, Dr, 16
Elbe River, 48
Emmaus Monastery, 126
Eton School, 12
Eupen and Malmedy, 21
Evian Conference, 27, 28, 35

Faires, Betty, 105
Faires, Leonard, 105
Faires, Nancy, 105
Faust House, 126
Fleischmann, Eva, 106
Fleischmann, Milena, 106
Florida, 130
Flynn, Errol, 130
Forres School, 66, 68, 69
France, 21, 27, 28, 90, 113, 114, 115, 117, 118, 119, 124
Frankfurt, 123

Geneva, 123
German Empire, 8, 22, 24
German Zeppelins, 9
Germany, 1, 6, 7, 15, 16, 18, 19, 20, 21, 24, 25, 28, 30, 31, 32, 35, 36, 37, 45, 48, 49, 71, 75, 78, 85, 88, 97, 98, 99, 100, 104, 106, 108, 110, 119, 124
Gestapo, 48–9, 89–92, 95–6, 99–101, 103
Gibson, Harold (Gibby), 88, 102
Gillies, William, 46–7, 62
Ginat, Josef, 107
Gissing, Vera, 1, 3–4, 37, 138
Gjelstrup, Grete *see* Winton, Grete
Glacier Foods, 131–2
Gloucestershire, 118
Gloucestershire Echo, 25
Gower, 46
Grand Hôtel Steiner, 46
Great Malvern, 41

Great War, the, *see* World War, First
Grenfell, David, 46–7, 53–4, 60
Grynszpan, Herschel, 35, 90
Gwyer, Barbara, 42

Hales, Harold, 59–61, 72
Hales Brothers, 59
Hales Trophy, 59
Hamburg, 15, 16, 17, 18, 19, 48
Hamburg University, 48
Hampstead, 6, 7, 8, 9, 10, 76, 112
Hampstead Borough Council, 112
Hanley, 59
Hardwick House, 133
Harrow School, 12
Harvard Law School, 124
Harwich, 1, 97, 101, 107
Hatfield, 118
Henlein, Konrad, 29–30
Hermannova Street, 44
Hertfordshire, 118
Hess, Myra, 82
Hess, Rudolf, 20, 23
Heston Aerodrome, 31
Himmler, Heinrich, 89, 109
Hindenburg, Paul Von, 22–3
Hitler, Adolf, 20–6, 28–32, 45, 48, 59, 80, 83–5, 88–9
Hodža, Milan, 42
Hohenberg, Duchess of, 8
Holland, 97, 98, 100, 101, 104, 106, 107
Holocaust, 2, 3, 5, 24, 123
Holocaust Memorial Day, 2
Hook of Holland, 1, 97, 101, 106, 107
Hotel Europa, 39
  see also Hotel Šroubek
Hotel Šroubek, 39
  see also Hotel Europa
House of Commons, 34, 47, 59
House of Windsor, 6

Ida (Aunt), 15
Illustrated London News, 119
India, 68
International Bank for Reconstruction and Development, 126

Index

International Committee for Refugees, 122, 126
Italy, 103
ITV, 4

Jaksch, Wenzel:
  meeting Doreen Warriner, 44–5
  fleeing to Prague, 45
  SSD Party, 45
  meeting with David Grenfell and William Gillies, 46
  friendship with Clement Attlee, 47
  escape from Prague, 112
  dinner party with the Wintons, 112
Japhet, 14
Judaism, ix, 2, 5, 7, 17, 24, 26, 27, 32, 34, 35, 36, 51, 57, 64, 77, 99, 107, 108, 109, 137, 138
Julius Baer Merchant Bank, 126
Jurisprudence, 68
Justitzová, Alice, 103
Justitzová, Mimka, 103

Karlsbader Programm, 30
Kennedy, John F., 124
Kidd, Ronald, 60
Kindertransport, 36, 37, 79
Kramer, Ann, 111
Kristallnacht, 35, 90

L. Behrens und Söhne, 15, 16, 18, 19
Lake District National Parks, 67
Lake Wannsee, 20
Landsberg Prison, 20
Lawrence, Guy, 131
Layton, Margaret, 74, 78, 101
Le Monnier, Bill *see* Barazetti, Bill
League of Nations, 21, 25
Leden, Judy, 134
Leden, Tom, 134
Lee, Rosalind, 80
Link Trainer, 118–19
Liverpool, 11
London, 1, 2, 7, 10, 11, 12, 14, 15, 17, 18, 20, 42, 46, 47, 49, 52, 61, 62, 63, 64, 74, 75, 76, 78, 82, 83, 85, 87, 90, 92, 97, 99, 100, 101, 102, 103, 104, 105, 107, 108, 113, 116, 119, 122, 137, 138
London Coliseum, 18
London County Council, 62
London Liverpool Street station, 1, 2, 85, 86, 87, 97, 101, 103, 104, 105, 107, 138
London School of Economics, 42
London Trade Council, 46
London Zoo, 103
Lord Mayor's Fund, 62
Lowyova, Vera, 104–105
Ludaks, 85
Luftwaffe, 114, 116, 118
Lyons, 132

MacDonald, Ramsay, 22
Maidenhead, 130, 131, 133
Maidenhead Borough Council, 133
Malvern Girls' College, 41
Manchester, 7
Manchester Evening News, 122
Manchester Guardian, 6
Marlborough College, 132
Maron, Hugo, 107
Maron, Rudy, 107
Marshall Plan, 127
Mary Somerville Research Fellowship, 42
Masaryk, Tomáš Garrigue, 4, 28, 89
Maxwell, Elizabeth, 3
Maxwell, Robert, 3
May, Theresa, 42
Mayer, Gerda, 71
Mein Kampf, 21, 23
Mencap, 133
MI6 *see* British Secret Intelligence Service
Mid-Sussex Times, 117
Mináč, Matej, 12, 81, 108
Ministry of Economic Welfare, 137
Mollusc, HMS, 135
Mommsenstrasse, 20
Mosley, Oswald, 14
Movement for the Care of Children from Germany, 75
Munich, 7, 24

Munich Agreement, 27, 31, 32, 59, 84, 102
Murdoch, Stanley, 10, 13, 129

National Council for Civil Liberties, 60
Nazi Party (National Socialist Party), ix, 2, 3, 16, 22, 25, 27, 29, 30, 31, 32, 33, 34, 36, 40, 45, 47, 48, 49, 50, 56, 57, 71, 73, 77, 78, 85, 87, 88, 90, 91, 92, 93, 97, 99, 100, 102, 103, 108, 119, 123, 124, 125, 126, 134
New Orleans, 130
New York Stock Exchange, 19
New York Times, 64
Newcastle Evening Chronicle, 93
Nicholas House, 133
Nicholas Winton's Lottery of Life, 81
Niven, David, 11
Nížkov village school, 33
Noel-Baker, Philip, 44, 46
North Schleswig, 21
North Sea, 1
Nottingham Journal, 113
Nuremberg, 7
Nuremberg Laws, 26

O'Malley, Elizabeth, 15–18, 20
Olympic Games (1940), 12
Operation Grün, 30
Order of Tomáš Garrigue Masaryk, 4
Oslo, 136
Oslo University Press, 136
Ottoman Empire, 8
Oxford, 41, 42, 67, 68, 103
Oxford University, 12, 41, 67, 68

Pall Mall Gazette, 22
Pan American, 43
Pankrác Prison, 103
Paris, 17, 20, 35, 37, 69, 89, 90, 126, 127, 128, 129
Parliament *see* House of Commons
Parliamentary Committee on Refugees, 60
Peace Pledge Union, 62
Pearl Harbor, 119

Penman, Mary, 44–6
Phelps, Geoff, 66, 71, 72, 75
Phelps, Guy, 135
Philby, Kim, 38
Philosophy, politics and economics, 41
Phoney War, 111–12
Pioneering Corps, 9
Plymouth, 115
Poland, 8, 28, 48, 54, 84, 108, 110, 112
Political Warfare Executive, 137
Prague, 1, 2, 33, 37, 38, 39, 40, 41, 42, 43, 44, 45, 46, 47, 48, 49, 51, 52, 53, 54, 59, 60, 61, 62, 63, 66, 68, 69, 71, 72, 73, 75, 76, 77, 78, 82, 83, 85, 86, 87, 88, 89, 90, 91, 93, 94, 95, 96, 98, 101, 102, 103, 104, 105, 106, 108, 111, 112, 120, 122, 123, 125, 126, 134, 135, 136, 137, 138
Prague Castle, 89
Prague National Theatre, 40
Pratt, Stanley, 133
Pride of Britain Award, 4
Princip, Gavrilo, 8
Proudhon, Pierre-Joseph, 129

Quakers, 44, 75
Queen Mary, RMS, 130

Rantzen, Esther, 3, 4
Rathbone, Eleanor, 59–61, 72
Red Cross, 33, 50, 73, 78, 111, 113, 114, 115, 117
Reed, Douglas, 87
Refugee Children's Movement, 36
Reisz, Karel, 86
Rhine River, 100
Rhineland, 25
Rockefeller Fellowship, 42
Ron, Amos, 104
Roosevelt, Eleanor, 124
Rosslyn Hill, 112–13
Route 65, 130
Roxburgh, J.F., 10, 11, 13
Royal Air Force (RAF), 117, 118, 119, 123, 135, 136
Royal Institute of International Affairs, 43

Royal Logistics Corps, 9
Rue de Passy, 129
Ruská Street, 104
Russia, 8, 21, 32, 137
Russian Empire, 8
Ruzyně Airport, 40

Saar Basin, 21, 24
Sala, Mr, 15, 17, 18
Salle Bertrand, 14
Samaritans, 133
Save the Children Fund, 43
Saxe-Coburg and Gotha family, 6
Schlesinger, Ernest, 106
Schlesinger, Joe, 106
School of Slavonic and East European Studies, 137
Schrecker, Frank, 102
Schrecker, Markéta, 103
Schrecker, Robert, 103
Schrecker, Tom, 102
Schwartz, Abba, 124
Scotland, 11
Sedbergh School, 67
Sherman, A.J., 35
Slough, 133–4
Slough Trading Estate, 133
Slovak People's Party, 85
Slovakia, 32, 84, 85, 86
Smith, Lyn, 34
South Cerney, 118–19
South Wales Evening Post, 80
Southampton, 136
Spitfire, 119
St Hugh's College, 41
St Hugh's Day, 42
St John Ambulance, 111–13
St Nazaire, 115
Staffordshire, 59
Stalin, Joseph, 32
Štěpánská Street, 43
Stopford, Robert, 90, 99, 137
Stowe School, 10–13, 15, 132
Sudeten German Party (SdP), 29, 31, 32
Sudeten Germans, 30, 43, 60, 97

Sudeten Social Democratic Party (SSD), 29, 112
Sudetenland, 21, 28, 29, 30, 31, 32, 34, 39, 45, 49, 84
Summerville College, 42
Sunday Mirror, 134
Surrey, 11
Sussex, 69, 115, 116, 117
Světlá Castle, 33
Swanage, 66, 70, 138
Switzerland, 27, 38, 47, 109, 123, 124, 129

Tanganyika, 68
Temple-Grenville, 10
Tennessee, Alabama, 130
That's Life!, 3–4
The Card, 59
The Guardian, 22
The Independent, 5
The Scotsman, 125
Theresienstadt Ghetto, 108, 109
Third Reich, 25, 30, 32, 84, 92
Tiso, Jozef, 84–5
Treaty of Versailles, 19, 21, 24, 31
Trinity College, Cambridge, 38

United Nations, 123, 137
United Nations Relief and Rehabilitation Administration, 137
University College London (UCL), 11, 12, 42, 137
University College School (UCS), 9
University of Heidelberg, 47

Valk, Herr and Frau, 16
Vienna, 41, 43
Vinohrady Synagogue, 126
vom Rath, Ernst, 35, 89
von Ribbentrop, Joachim, 30
Voršilská Street, 94, 100

Walder, Peter, 71
Wales, 46
War of the Worlds, 60
Warner Brothers, 130

Warriner, Doreen:
 birth, 41
 upbringing, 41
 academics, 41–2
 Mary Somerville Research Fellowship, 42
 lecturing, 42
 awarded Rockefeller Fellowship, 42
 arrival in Prague, 40, 43, 44
 views on the Quakers, 44
 relationship with Wenzel Jaksch, 44, 45, 46
 meeting David Grenfell and William Gillies, 46
 joining the BCRC, 47
 concern about child refugees, 51
 children's section of the BCRC, 51–2, 54
 accompanying refugees out of Czechoslovakia, 54
 creating lists, 54
 tours of refugee camps, 60
 controversial letter to the *Daily Telegraph*, 61
 frustrations with the BCRC, 62
 praise for Nicholas Winton, 52, 63–4, 74, 122–3
 meeting Trevor Chadwick, 66, 71
 letter to Nicolas Winton, 87
 pornography in office, 91–2
 leaving Prague, 92
 reunion in Prague, 126
 referral letter for Nicolas Winton, 122–3
 working for the Ministry of Economic Welfare, 137
 receiving an OBE, 137
 re-joining the University College London, 137
 death, 137
 posthumous recognition, 138
Warwickshire, 41
Waugh, Evelyn, 11
Weidner, Jean, 129
Weigl, Willi, 71
Wellington, Beatrice, 101

Wells, H.G., 60
Wenceslas Square, 39, 43, 51, 89
Wertheim, Babette (Nicholas's mother) *see* Winton, Barbara
Wertheim, Bruno, 7
Wertheim, Charlotte, 7
Wertheim, Hannah, 7
Wertheim, Nicholaus, 7
Wertheim, Rudolf (Nicholas's father) *see* Winton, Rudolf
Wertheim, Sasha, 7
West Indies, 42
West Prussia, 21
Westminster School, 12, 38
Wexham Park Hospital, 134
White Waltham Airfield, 134
Willis, Barbara, 76
Willow Road, 76, 87, 112
Wilson, Woodrow, 95
Wilson Station, 95, 96, 99, 104, 105, 106, 138
Windsor, 133
Winton, Barbara (Nicholas's mother):
 upbringing, 7
 meeting Rudolf, 7
 wedding, 7
 religion, 7
 moving to Britain, 8
 name change from Wertheim, 6
 children, 6, 9
 First World War, 8–9
 travelling to Germany with Winton, 15
 letters from Nicholas, 19, 51, 53, 58, 60, 61, 63, 74, 120
 researching refugee policy, 53
 working for the BCRC, 76
 greeting trains, 86–7, 98, 100, 101, 103, 104, 105, 108
 post rescue children's organisation, 110
 dinner with Wenzel Jaksch, 112
 helping Nicholas get a job, 130
 deteriorating relationship with Nicholas, 131
Winton, Barbara (Nicholas's daughter), 7, 131–2

Index

Winton, Grete:
  first meeting with Nicholas, 127–8
  sightseeing around Paris, 128
  marriage proposal, 129
  wedding, 129
  honeymoon in the United States, 130
  family home in Maidenhead, 131–2
  birth of their three children, 131
  discovering scrapbook, 3
  deteriorating relationship with Nicholas's mother, 131
  death of Robin, 132
  support for Mencap, 133
  death, 134
Winton, Nicholas:
  birth, 6
  siblings, 6, 9
  name change from Wertheim, 6
  growing up in Hampstead, 8
  family wealth, 8
  education, 9–14
  religion, 6–7, 13, 17, 26, 64–5, 111
  memories of First World War, 8–9
  schooling, 9, 10, 11, 12, 13, 14, 132
  sport, 11, 12, 13
  fencing, 12, 14, 20, 128
  pigeon fancying, 11, 12
  early career, 14, 15, 52–3
  relationship with Elizabeth O'Malley, 15, 16, 17, 18, 20
  views on drinking, 16
  relationship with Gretschen, 16–17, 20
  social life in Germany, 16, 20
  New Year 1930 celebrations, 18
  Hitler's rise to power, 21, 22, 24–7, 31, 32
  uprising in the Sudetenland, 31
  Czech refugee camps, 33, 72
  pacifism, 27, 111
  decision to travel to Prague, 38–9
  returning to Hotel Europa, 39
  meeting Doreen Warriner, 40, 43, 50
  reflections on Bill Barazetti, 50
  British Committee for Refugees from Czechoslovakia (BCRC), 47, 50–1
  concern about child refugees, 51
  children's section of the BCRC, 51–3, 55, 74, 78
  working with other aid organisations, 55
  letters from his mother, 19, 51, 53, 57, 58, 60, 61, 63, 74, 120, 130
  meeting with parents, 55, 63, 72
  language capability, 56
  meeting Harold Hales, 59
  comments about Eleanor Rathbone, 60
  witnessing his first rescue, 64
  relationship with Trevor Chadwick, 66, 68, 71, 72
  being followed in Prague, 73
  return flight to England, 75
  first air rescue, 75
  building a team in London, 76
  second air rescue, 76–7, 80
  third air rescue, 77
  air rescue to Sweden, 78
  news reports, 79–80, 93
  gathering potential foster parents, 80–3
  complementing the British authorities, 83
  first train rescue, 85–7
  second train rescue, 95–8
  third train rescue, 98–100
  fourth train rescue, 100–101
  fifth train rescue, 101–103
  sixth train rescue, 103–104
  seventh train rescue, 104–105
  eighth train rescue, 105–108
  forging official documents, 98–9
  cancelled train, 108
  post rescue children's organisation, 110
  letter to Doreen Warriner, 111
  quitting banking, 111, 122
  work with St John Ambulance, 111–13
  joining the Red Cross, 113
  inspected by the King, 113
  deployment to France, 114
  posting in Sussex, 115–17
  time with the RAF, 117–21
  passenger in a Spitfire, 119

reflections of Europe during the war, 119, 123
joining the International Committee for Refugees, 122–6
reunion in Prague, 126
joining the International Bank for Reconstruction and Development, 126–30
moving to Paris, 127
job with Glacier Foods, 131–2
family home in Maidenhead, 131–2
birth of their three children, 131
deteriorating relationship with his mother, 131
death of Robin, 132
retirement, 132
entering politics, 133
support for Mencap, 133
charity work in later life, 133
entering the public domain, 134
modesty, ix, 129
getting old, ix, 132
rescued children's descendants, x, 138
honours, 2, 4, 5, 133–4
scrapbook, 3
That's Life!, 3–4, 139
death of Grete, 134
turning 100, 134
death, 134, 138
posthumous recognition of Trevor Chadwick, 136–7
Winton, Nick (Nicholas's son), 73, 81, 99, 105, 131, 132

Winton, Robin (Nicholas's son), 131
Winton, Rudolf:
   birth, 7
   struggles with parent's death, 7
   moving to Britain, 8
   meeting Babette, 7
   wedding, 7
   religion, 7
   name change from Wertheim, 6
   children, 6, 9
   First World War, 8–9
   rejection from the military, 9
   health, 9
   joining Pioneering Corps, 9
   career, 14, 29
   travelling, 15
Winton Cup, 12
Winton House, 133
Wood, Edward (Lord Halifax), 60
Worcestershire, 41
Wordsworth, Elizabeth, 41
Wordsworth, William, 41
World War, First, 6, 8, 9, 11, 14, 21, 26, 28, 29, 43, 60, 92
World War, Second, ix, 12, 47, 108, 136

Yorkshire Dales, 67
Yugoslavia, 137

Zenkl, Petr, 33